RAISED
IN CAPTIVITY

"The Christian ideal
has not been tried
and found wanting.
It has been found difficult,
and left untried."

—G. K. Chesterton

Also by C. McNair Wilson

*YHWH Is Not a Radio Station in Minneapolis and Other Things
Everyone Should Know* (HarperSanFrancisco, 1983)

*Everyone Wants to Go to Heaven, But.../ Wit, Faith, and a Light
Lunch* (PageMill Press, 2000)

YES, AND... Brainstorming Secrets of a Theme Park Designer
(AmperBang Press, 2003)

RAISED IN CAPTIVITY

A Memoir of a Life Long Churchaholic

C. McNair Wilson

Jet Cadet, Retired

Illustrated by
McNair

A Crossroad Carlisle Book
The Crossroad Publishing Company
New York

The Crossroad Publishing Company
481 Eighth Avenue, New York, NY 10001

This book is typeset in 11/15 ITC Stone Informal.
The display type is La Bamba.

Printed in the United States of America

Library of Congress Cataloging-in-Publication Data
Wilson, C. McNair.
    Raised in captivity : memoir of a life long churchaholic /
C. McNair Wilson ; illustrated by McNair.
       p.   cm.
    "A Crossroad Carlisle book."
    Includes bibliographical references and index.
    ISBN 0-8245-2118-8 (alk. paper)
    1. Wilson, C. McNair–Humor. 2. Christian life–United
States–Humor. 3. Church membership–United States–Humor.
4. Christian biography–United States–Humor.   I. Title.
BR1725.W49A3 2003
277.3'082'092–dc21

                                                    2003007256

1 2 3 4 5 6 7 8 9 10   10 09 08 07 06 05 04 03

For Todd,
my brother,
who lived most of this
with me,
but more quietly.

DWIGHT —

You are
NOT
your past.

Cynthia Likson

We do not know with a certainty how much humor there is in Christ's teaching, but we can be sure that there is far more than is normally recognized. In any case, there are numerous passages in the recorded teaching which are practically incomprehensible when regarded as sober prose, but which are luminous once we become liberated from the gratuitous assumption that Christ never laughed.

—Elton Trueblood, *The Humor of Christ*

Contents

11

McNair's Preface
(The part no one reads)

The wish to be told a story
never dies in the human heart.

—Robertson Davies, *The Merry Heart*

No one reads the Preface to a book. That's what my editor and lots of other publishing folks tell me. Too bad. It's in the Preface that the author lays out the plan, the promise, if you will, of the book. Here a clear and certain objective is stated—or should be. Most of my objective, the why of this book, is outlined in the first story, "Organ Prelude."

I want to use this space to give you some ground rules and working definitions for the way these stories are told.

"The church I grew up in" is the most frequently used phrase in this book. Here I am not referring to any particular denomination or congregation. I grew up in many different flavors and will tell you about them. I use "the church" to mean the universal body of believers who study, worship, and celebrate their faith in any number of congregations organized under dozens of names. "Church" in these pages has come to mean gatherings of Christians—both Protestant and Roman Catholic—as well as Jewish believers. This book and my stories are a remembrance—a memoir, not a biography—of being raised in and around true believers devout in faith and resolute in their practices. Sometimes those practices were drawn from instructions from their Creator as found in the Holy Bible. Too often, though, we received bonus rules and extra procedures developed from cultural proclivities and an unceasing penchant to "get it right." This was more about not embarrassing the church than about serving God.

There's the rub. We try so hard, too hard, to please our Maker, by enforcing models for thinking and doing on young believers (or pre-believers) to get them to fall in line according to our biases. The God of Abraham — revered by Christians, Jews, and Moslems — is very clear that it is *not* about what we do, it is about being, *how* we do it.

The Spirit of God is not only a living entity, but also, I believe, the intentionality of God. We often speak of the letter of the law — what the law actually says — and the spirit of the law, too. I believe there is also a "spirit of the law" with God's law as well.

The Bible says it is by our fruits that true believers will be known. Saint Paul (a Jew and a citizen of Rome) puts it best when he drops a note to the church in Galatia to tell them that just like a tree bears fruit, a life guided by God's Spirit also has fruit. He lists the fruits of the Spirit: "affection for others, patience, peaceful demeanor, exuberance about life, serenity, loyal commitments, compassion, and a conviction that a basic holiness permeates things and people." He even says hospitality is a spiritual gift. (I know that's right as I have stayed in homes that did not have the gift of hospitality.) Paul does not say that some of these fruits are only for men and others are only for women. Nor are they bound by age, culture, or race. Further, he says that there is no law against any of these.

In Eugene Peterson's deft setting of the New Testament, called *The Message,* he goes on to restate Paul's position against a life governed by rules — do's and don'ts — like this.

"Legalism is helpless in bringing this about. It only gets in the way." Exactly.

This book is about church stuff that got in the way of me being me. It's not about what's wrong with any particular denomination, though the wry humor that filled my family's conversations was a means of coping with the bumps in the parking lot of faith, and it appears throughout these pages. If you bump into a sarcastic statement about a particular denomination, I apologize. I can't get to *all* of them, so feel free to insert the name of your church at any point. (It will work. I promise.) In more than three decades of speaking at churches, conferences, and colleges, I have learned that the denominations are more alike than different. If Christians actually practiced this—lived it—their harmony would be deafening.

Even Christian and Jew have more in common with each other than with the atheist or more banal agnostic. Sister Corita's poster from the 1960s got this right, and best:

"Not to believe is to believe."

This book is about believing—deeply, richly, and fully. I believe, and I believe that the church—the organized faith institution—has too often created roadblocks to that full, abundant life in the Spirit. If you have experienced road-blocks to your faith — or a full body block from a church leader—read on. If you are a church leader, take off your shoulder pads of demanding doctrine, remove your helmet of heady, impractical certainty, get rid of all your Gospel Gear and read on.

Find a comfortable chair, grab a favorite pen for marginal musings and misgivings, and slide some Copland,

Yo Yo Ma, or McFerrin into the discola. Pour yourself a goblet of Nazareth Vineyard's "End of the Wedding Red" and enter McNair's Side Show of Orthodox Oddities.

Chances are you'll find a bit of your own story in some of mine.

Read on!

1

Organ Prelude
Why I wrote this book

In the great hand of God I stand.

—*Macbeth*, Act ii, sc. 3 (Banquo)

Make no mistake about it, my family was a Bible-reading, hymns-out-of-the-hymnal-singing, missionary-supporting, Christian-school-attending, choir-joining, scripture-verse-memorizing, summer-camp-going, tithe-giving, big-giant-Christmas-pageant-performing, Wednesday-night-prayer-meeting-praying, church-league-basketball-playing, Holy-Spirit-(or Ghost)-believing, God-fearing, gospel-magic-and-ventriloquism-doing, twenty-seventh-generation, going-out-after-the-Sunday-night-service-for-pie-eating, Jesus-loving, churchgoing family. And we didn't play cards and we didn't go to movies on Sundays neither!

My family has been going to church for so long that our family tree is a flannel graph story and the family Bible is in German—Old Testament German.

At age four, I was sprinkled by the Methodists; at twelve, I was immersed by the Babtists (that's double "B," Babtists); at sixteen, I left the church of my parents' choice and joined a non-denominational church where they stood us in the parking lot and hosed us down. At nineteen, I joined a Presbyterian church — owing to my love of the bagpipe.

The Presbyterians formed a committee about me that is still meeting to this day. The last fifteen years or so I have been hanging out and worshiping in buildings marked "E-piscopalian."

I have spoken, taught, and performed in churches, conferences, and colleges of every brand that I have ever heard of and several I had not heard of before or since.

Growing up in my house was all about going to church and going everywhere else with folks who went to church. To say we were religiously addicted doesn't even come close. We were churchaholics.

I was raised in captivity.

Tonight on A&E Biography

This is not a biography. 'Tis a memoir of critical parts of my spiritual upbringing. These are all true stories, and they are all my stories. Everyone tried to contribute, telling me their horror stories from growing up in religiously addicted families, but I could only write about the person seated in my pew.

After the first few lines of this book stumbled out of my fountain pen one afternoon in a restaurant on the San Francisco Bay, the challenging task of remembering began. Specifically, I wanted to remember growing up in the American subcontinent of Churchianity. More importantly, I wanted to think about who I became because I was there. This is the story of becoming and unbecoming me as a result of a life in and around church and church folk. More importantly, it is about what I was thinking and feeling during those early years when virtually all of life grew out of our church life.

Feeling. Everywhere you turn, there's a "gathering of men," or a "women's issues" group, and just about everybody I know is either in counseling, getting into counseling, thinking about getting into counseling, or thinking that they will never get out of counseling. Counseling is what church folk call emotional and psychological assistance — therapy. Mostly, church folk don't call for help. They merely pray about it or, just as often, we tell each other to "snap out of it." Often, too, we say, I have a book you should read.

Raised in Captivity is the story of the events that we somehow don't snap out of — not very easily, anyway, and not very quickly. We have to work at it. This book is the stories of my work and it is the work itself. You may be working to get out of church. I want you to stay in the church or come back — even if you left years ago. We need you. You and me, we *are* the church — the family of God. This ill-assorted contingent of believers and seekers is the ragtag army of God, an assemblage of misfits and foundlings shuffling toward Zion.

A therapist friend says, "I'm not about telling folks that they're sick or well. I work with people who are stuck and want to get unstuck." Eventually, life is about recovering from the events that scared us down the wrong rabbit hole to where we find ourselves now. Stuck.

Here, then, is my journey back inside the "church me" of an earlier time. It is about getting stuck and trying to get unstuck on the stuff of Churchianity, God, and the too many people and institutions telling me exactly what to do or precisely how to believe. For years, life was a series of choices that had to be made based solely on belief in God. Those choices build the character for which we are held accountable. There is the daily judgment of a loving, frustrated, and disappointed Creator. 'Twas, though, a God redefined and

interpreted by the church—the family of God—as a more angry and ogre-like overseer.

This church "family" of mine, I began to realize, was in trouble. The structure is all out of whack, the kids have been leaving "home" in loaded Land Rovers. The value system— once worth dying for—has been redecorated to harmonize with the modern tastes found in this morning's *USA Today* or tonight's MTV. Faith has been repainted so many times that no one remembers the original palette. It's even lost its original shape. Oh, that "worth dying for" part, well, that kind of commitment died out long ago. These days the best we can get out of members of God's family is that there are a few things worth arguing about.

In the Sean Connery film *The Name of the Rose,* poor monks debate rich monks about whether or not Jesus owned the clothes He wore. My first thought was, these monks — on both sides — would have gotten along quite nicely in the churches I grew up in. They were as entertaining as they were shallow, trite, and embarrassing.

Besides being troubled, the family of God that I grew up in was in a constant state of appeasement. They bent over backwards — and broke in half a few times — to cover their tracks any time one among us misstepped, misspoke, or "mistaked." It was in the church that I learned that "the bigger you are, the harder you fall" and the more dynamic you bounce back. You could write a Third Testament on prominent preachers who "fell from grace" and returned to preach, publish, pass the plate, profligate, and profit from their pious prose, proudly proclaiming their "mendacities" over the airwaves. It's as if their misdeeds were a gift, given to them from on high — their very own forty days in the wilderness. Adultery, greed, and avarice — every kind of institutional skullduggery has sliced through the family of God and all of us apologized for these scoundrels. They are not our fault. That we continue to keep them in high places, though, is our responsibility. We have passionately proclaimed their innocence with ignorance and fear. When we weren't pleading their innocence, we were blindly defending these errant men o' the cloth because they were stressed, overworked, or any number of other flimsy excuses. If the pastor has sinned, we fear there might be no God. We live in abject terror of the failure of our leaders. Meanwhile, Jesus was nailed to the cross before, during, and after we were paying attention to his sacrifice for our self-ishness, our egos, and our villainy. "In that, while we were yet pastors, teachers, evangelists, and churchacrats, Christ died for us." He forgives us our stupidity as we must forgive those who are stupid against and amongst us.

A healthy family faces the abusive, excessive, or addicted family member and, refusing to ignore and cover up their addiction, they confront them and demand recovery and healing. The church is not a museum for saints and ex-super sinners. It is a hospital for the addicted who need recovering from their misuse and abuse of the very Creator in whose name they carry on so bumblingly.

As often as I have been angered by my church family, I have been entertained by them. More often I have been helped and enriched. Herein, I seek to be at once a comedic confession of our asinine abuses and an analysis-by-anecdote toward reclamation. Come with me on a journey through my spiritual past with more than a few giggles about where the family of God has gotten stuck along the way. My church family seems to be getting unstuck a little more everyday.

Bring a shovel.

2

A Confession

"The Wilsons, they're churchgoers"

My way of joking is to tell the truth.
It's the funniest joke in the world.

—George Bernard Shaw

I'm an Evangelical. My mother and father were Evangelicals. Even my grandparents—on all three sides (don't ask)—were Evangelicals. I am an "Adult Child of Evangelicals."

Back in my grandparents' day, they didn't know enough about this particularly American-bred religion to give it a name. Nonetheless, a lot of folks did it. A lot. It was usually referred to in simpler, whispered tones: "The Wilsons? Oh, they're churchgoers."

Those most ardent about their churchgoing called themselves "fundamentalists." Their whole lives revolved around going to church, God, and what the Bible says about it. "It" means everything. Fundamentalists can come up with a verse, or a small chunk of words forming a partial verse, for just about every activity and subject in life. If the Bible didn't say something about something, well then, it was nothing and the fundamentalists just wouldn't talk about it.

Funnily enough, fundamentalists could most often be heard talking about subjects on which the Bible had very little—or nothing—to say.

There are still a lot of fundamentalists around today. They are the hard-core, "nobody's-right-but-us" Evangelical believers. They talk a lot about subjects on which the Bible has little to say.

Seems like I've been an Evangelical all my life. At least I've been doing the stuff that is now termed "Evangelical" all my life. All the churches that I grew up in were filled with folks who were avid readers, students, and believers of the entire Bible—both the Old and New Testaments. Their focus, indeed their emphasis, for virtually every church activity was evangelism, calling new believers to the gospel—winning new converts. We called it witnessing, winning the lost, reaching the unsaved. The "unsaved" are often referred to as non-Christians (a word I grew to loath.) For most of my life—actually, for all of my life—I attended churches every Sunday, camp every summer, and private, church-related school every day. Mostly I liked it all at the time—and have great memories of it to this day.

All my friends growing up were Evangelicals except for one family in our Pasadena, California, neighborhood. The Clarks were non-Evangelicals. More specifically, they were Jehovah's Witnesses. Back then—I was ten—I wasn't exactly sure what that was. At first I thought they were like grown-up Boy Scouts who went door-to-door selling their *Watch Tower* magazines.

We learned right off that there were two noticeable differences between Jehovah's Witnesses and Evangelicals.

First, Jehovah's Witnesses do not say the Pledge of Allegiance to the American flag in school, or anywhere else. They told me that the Bible said not to swear any oaths, and they showed me the exact verse in the Bible that said that. One whole verse. At that point I suggested to my

folks that they might be fundamentalists. They were not fundamentalists.

(There are what I call "one-verse Christians" who take an adamant, unwavering stand on one verse in the Bible and judge all others by their stance on that one verse. My dad taught me that when God has something important to teach us, it can be found many places in the Bible. If it's only in one verse, it might not be God's most important point.)

The second obvious difference between us and the Jehovah's Witnesses was that when playing at our house, no one was allowed to say "shut up." No one. If they did, they were sent home. The Jehovah's Witnesses kids were sent home, often. It's not that "shut up" was a dirty word or "swear word." It was rude. Evangelicals and other Christians shouldn't be rude. No one should be rude. "Shut up" wasn't the only thing you could do that was rude, but being told that God doesn't want us to be rude covers a lot of stuff. In some ways, teaching us about "rude" was a big lesson to learn cause it covered a lot. Trying to teach us every single thing that was rude — one rude thing at a time — would have taken years. I learned "rude" as an overall concept early and quickly. Fundamentalists, meanwhile, teach one thing at a time and seem to be constantly inventing new things that the old fundamentalists tell the young fundamentalists are against the rules. (There actually are "young fundamentalists.") These rules are called "legalism." It is the strictest form of fundamentalism. It is the dark side of Christianity.

Growing up in church wasn't strange or uncomfortable or odd. It's like my friend who has triplets. "How do you do it?" everyone gasps. But triplets is not unusual for her and her husband. Triplets is all they've ever known. For me, being an American, Protestant, Evangelical churchgoer, with Evangelical parents, church friends, and relatives, attending a private church-related school and all those different brands of Protestant churches was normal. Sure, I knew there were others who didn't go to church at all. I even saw an Atheist on television a couple of times. But my world was church families of all sizes and shapes—most of them pretty normal folks. Or so they seemed at the time.

Our family was not oblivious to other faiths. Indeed, my mother was fascinated with the traditions of the Jewish faith and used some in her schoolteaching. She had been raised in the Episcopal church and my father in the Baptist church. We were forever discussing denominationalism and world

26

faiths. I knew about Buddhists, Moslems, Jews, Atheists, Native American Shamans, Mormons, Jehovah's Witnesses, Christian Scientists, Quakers, Mennonites, Covenanters, Baptists/Presbyterians/Methodists, Lutherans, Evangelical Free folk, Pentecostals and Charismatics (though I still can't tell those two apart), Plymouth Brethren, snake-handlin'-down-by-the-river-Baptists, Humanists, Shintoists, Hindus, Freemasons, Nudists (family friends,) Gnostics, and Agnostics. (Raise your hand if I forgot anyone.) Since my folks were educators, we really did discuss all of these and more.

It was not until much later—well, maybe fourth or fifth grade, but it seemed later—that I became aware of the fact that I was actually a real, live Evangelical. I hated being categorized back then, and I hate it even more now. It was back then that I started to realize that being a churchgoer was different. It was a minority that only a decade or so later would become a very noisy majority — even though they would call themselves the "silent majority." This Evangelical minority I found myself a part of was not like being a person of color. No, being Evangelical was sort of like being left-handed. Imagine being left-handed *and* Evangelical.

I am.

Before we draw any conclusions, let me draw you a picture of growing up in a churchgoing family. It includes journeys out of and back into the Evangelical subculture. There's been more than one round trip. Attempts at any but the most flimsy and whimsical definition of "Evangelical" I will leave up to those theologians in their ceaseless attempts at systematizing things eternal and non-systematic. (Don't they ever get out and just go to a ball game?) I will, though, offer stories from my life presented for your consideration as a journey into the Evangelical Zone.

Here is a place where humankind in the mid- to late twentieth century battled over the Bible; sang great music, but rarely danced; wrote too much bad music; talked; "shared"; conferred; retreated, but never advanced. We preached, broadcast, and boycotted all in a mad rush to define, contain, package, market, and manage the indefinable. "God in a box," as J. B. Phillips keenly observed. Evangelicalism, if it was anything, was western civilization and westernized civilizations putting God in a suit and tie, "laying on" a shave and a haircut, and teaching "him" (God) the Pledge of Allegiance to the American flag, a front-door-sales-pitch and an MTV beat. This, then, is what I did as a follower after Bethlehem's Star. Sometimes I did it because I deeply, sincerely believed—and was committed. Too many times I acted on the instruction and even the "orders" of the "present authority" over me. They told me that this is righteousness, do this. Those were the times when the spiritual road less traveled became a four-lane super-highway with the church bus mindlessly cruise-controlling to Zion.

"Wait a minute, Slow down! I think I just saw an injured person back there on the side of the road."

"Where? A what? I didn't see anything."

"We just passed them. Shouldn't we stop and help?"

"Oh, I love this song! Turn up the radio. Yeah!"

3

A Comedy of Terrors
There was always laughter

You have as much laughter as you have faith.

—Martin Luther

My father danced at my wedding. In all my thirty-five years I had never seen my father dance—not even kidding around, which he did with every other activity in life. My mom and I had been dancing with each other for years. All my life has been filled with music and dancing and art and theatre, and comedy. And church. Church was always music, rarely theatre, but it has always been comedy—to me and my family. We laughed till it hurt, till we cried. A good laugh can be at once the most severe and enjoyable pain. We've all had experiences that were painful while they're happening, and we say, "You'll laugh about this someday." And we do. We say, "Oh sure, you laugh now, but while it was happening, . . ." as we shake our heads and laugh.

Around the Wilson house, though, we laughed *while* life was happening. Certainly as church was happening we laughed. We need a bumper sticker proclaiming *Church Happens!* Sometimes, during the most gruesome miscarriages of faith, we looked past misplaced passions and saw the silliness. We found clarity beyond the moment and lived through it, because it was so preposterous and so

29

terrifying that we were dumfounded, stunned. Observing the actions of the church, our fellow believers, and the corporate foolishness of church leadership rendered us at once traumatized, powerless, and thoroughly entertained. We found ourselves so debilitated by things done and things left undone—in the name of God—that we sat, at a (short) distance, watching. It was a great amusement— a grand gogol.

Often, we laughed at ourselves to the extent that we were a part of it all.

Regaled with laughter over the monumental lack of thought on the part of the spokespersons of our faith, we lived through an ongoing tour de faith of slapstick comedy masquerading as spiritual piety. Like the too many cartoons of da Vinci's *Mona Lisa* with a hastily drawn mustache scribbled in, the church is too often a familiar painting of Christ with a big red clown nose. The church careening and colliding into itself in one continuous mad dash, a gospel goose chase down the righteous road less traveled. It's a new ride at the carnival: Bumper Belief. In their relentless attempts to speak for God, people have too often spoken words antithetical to God's heart. Just as often, they neglected to speak words God has already spoken and called us to put into action.

We complained about welfare fraud and expended no effort to assist the most needy just down the street from our churches. We disparaged civil rights activists and did nothing to embrace God's broad spectrum of people groups in our services. We decried the filthy, homeless "bums" in the streets and offered them no place to shower, eat, or sleep. Too much of this bellyaching (my dad's term) still emanates from pulpits and programs on TV and radio. The cost of just the overly opulent "visitors center" at one popular ministry headquarters could build the homes of a hundred families through Habitat for Humanity.

To grow up in the church was to be a part of an epic comedy as innocuous as any episode of *Seinfeld* — and also "about nothing." This was also a tragedy of biblical proportions. Not, though, the tragedy of William Shakespeare's sad kings, but Evangelicalism's self-made monarchs of the air waves with their gravity-defying hair waves. Growing up raised in the captivity of the church was more like Groucho, Chico, and Harpo spending a day at the churches.

We were at odds with our culture on the demonic lyrics of heavy metal music and the decadence of the two-piece bathing suit. Christians, or more specifically Roman Catholics and Protestants, share a basic belief in the historic, human Christ of the Newer Testament walking among us while, at the same time, we squabble over the seating arrangement of Christ's disciples, the job description of his mother, and the alcohol content (if any) of the wine list at the Last Supper. Add to all this Christian carrying on the eight million Jews who share with Catholics and Protestants an abiding faith in the God of Abraham, Sarah, and Eden, and the theological conflict moves on to the battlefield of life.

The laughter stopped when the comedy turned cruel. When the stuff of faith became an excuse for bad manners. I was nauseated when church leadership — some of God's closest friends — said AIDS was God's revenge on the immorality of our times; suggested that to fight communism in Southeast Asia was to fight atheism in the cosmos; or when both teams prayed before a Super Bowl game — captured by the network cameras for all the world to see — it was clear, at least to the winning coach, that God was on their side, "Cuz we won!"

The family of God reached new heights of comedic idiocy when the only issue that Catholics and Protestants of every flavor in the greater Los Angeles area rallied together around in thirty years was their public protest over an otherwise insignificant event: the release of the film *The Last Temptation of Christ*. It was, by any standards, a less-than-excellent movie, made monumentally important by a press conference that was sillier than any *Saturday Night Live* sketch could have been. I was happy that my minister, though invited, boycotted the boycott of the movie. He was probably doing something foolish that day like feeding the hungry or visiting a hospitalized church member with AIDS or simply crafting next Sunday's liturgy.

That press conference, too, was terrifying, and I never laughed so hard. I watched as acquaintances of mine, on the evening news coverage, railed against the film as if they were personally arm wrestling the Prince of Darkness. Instead it was a spitting match against the straw people. (Later, I asked a couple of "friends" on that panel of the theologically ticked-off just how many tickets they actually sold to *Last Temptation?* I'm certain that the curiosity factor alone—about their protest—was responsible for thousands of extra tickets purchased. When I went to see the film, I talked to thirteen people in line ahead and behind me and everyone had come "to see what all the fuss was about." Now how can I organize a boycott against this book?)

More tragedy: When I was growing up, we had an assistant minister who used his once-a-month moment in the pulpit (Sunday evening service only) to wax venomous against the practice of going to movies—any movie. Once, in the early sixties, he used "101 Damnations" as a sermon title. (He later donated his brain to the Green Giant company to be soaked in butter sauce.)

I experienced the complete terror of almost being kicked out of private school for the crime of being the person I believed God had created, and my parents had raised me, to be. At that very legalistic (strict), private, church-related school it was against their rules for me to be "me." Twenty-four years later, I was finally able to find laughter in remembering those years. My mother, while sifting through the collected debris of our lives before moving with my dad to their retirement villa-by-the-sea, found key documents from those events. We laughed, finally, at the letters exchanged between my dad and that school board regarding my role as a student leader or student rabble-rouser.

The comedy is everywhere. A woman involved in an on-campus ministry at a major university told me and my co-workers in a Christian street theatre company that comedy had no place in the life of True Believers. A favorite running gag is the scores of Christian colleges that do not allow on-campus smoking, while serving nutritionally vapid and destructive meals in the cafeteria. These are the stories of my life in the family of God. They are the funny and frightening events that I have remembered, rejected, and am recovering from in the comedy of terrors found in a religiously devout and addicted family.

The regimen for recovering from being an adult child of Evangelicals is a thirteen-step program. The extra step is tap dancing. If you were raised Nazarene — or any one of the many "No Dancing" denominations — the program allows you to simply move your toes up and down inside your shoes, so no one knows you're dancing.

I hope this book will be mostly comedy, and that the laughter will be gentle medicine for any terrors of today that still occur in the family of God — especially for all of those raised in captivity.

4

Taking the Shepherds Upstairs
And other Christmas traditions

And there were in the same country shepherds abiding
in the field, keeping watch over their flock by night.

—The Gospel of Luke 2:8

It was my brother Todd's turn to hide the Baby Jesus. After
all, he'd earned it. Hiding the Baby Jesus was a rite, a tradition. It could only be earned. The act of "hiding" was
an intellectual as well as a psychological exercise. It had
become an art form and a science.

The Program

The weekend of Thanksgiving my dad would start hauling out the boxes marked "Christmas decorations" from
the basement, attic, or garage. The first box we always
opened every year was the one marked "Nativity." It was
the manger, or, as my mom always called it, the crèche.
We would open this most important of all Christmas boxes,
this timeworn and oft-repaired relic, and find old friends
all neatly "swaddled" in tissue paper left over from Christmas gifts past: the original cast returning for yet another
tabletop tableau. Our very own Oberammergau passion
play, in miniature, which we took on the road from Minnesota to Los Angeles, to Pasadena, to San Jose, and to

San Diego. Shepherds and sheep, three wise men (the biblically correct number), one camel, the Christmas Angel, Mary, Joseph, the donkey, one cow (lowing), and the now famous, soon-to-be-in-hiding Baby Jesus — all present and accounted for.

The baby was the main character in our story. For our family, displaying these factory-made figures was as much about telling the story of Christmas as it was about public celebration of our faith. It had design, reason, and meaning: the simple story of eternity interrupting human history.

We began by setting the stage: placing the manger on the entry hall table. Our "crèche," though wooden, dark, and covered with bits of straw that had been glued to it at the factory, was a bit too nice at first. We set about to rough it up, age it, distress it, make it more run down — a place unbecoming God. It was the place behind the place where travelers stayed in a do-nothing little town. Out beyond "out back" was the manger — a stable. Here eternity and mortality would collide one cold morning just after 4:00 a.m. Here, too, human history would be changed forever by the first cry of a baby — a Jewish boy baby from working-class parents, the distant relations of their nation's poet king. Another shepherd in the line of David.

No one really expected such inauspicious beginnings, such deliberately dreadful digs for the maternity ward of the Deity come-among-us. The world expects the arrival of kings and monarchs to be accompanied by pomp and pageantry. Not here. This advent was to be different. Simple, unceremonious. More unnoticed than noticed.

For this particular birth of the Messiah, however, God chose the highway less paved. They came in the middle of the night, disguised as a very young, very pregnant teenage girl and her furniture maker boyfriend. A couple cold and lost in the night. Strangers in a strange town, they showed up on a holiday weekend — without reservations. God sneaked in the back door of history, through the servants' entrance.

Next, some local sheepherders were invited by sending a Western Union employee to drive out into the hills, honking his horn and flashing his one remaining head light on high beam. He did a singing telegram of the "Hallelujah Chorus" — assisted by a half dozen other vocalists following in an old Dodge pickup truck. The shepherds, awakened from their not-very-deep sleep on that frozen, rocky hillside, grabbed a couple of smallish over-their-shoulder lambs (for atmosphere) and hightailed it into town. Finding the young family, they realized that this was at once the right place and completely the wrong place for the birthplace of the Promised One.

Later, and we don't know if it was days or months after the birth, but...later, to be sure, came Kings — big, smart adult kings—and their substantial retinues of servants and caravan creatures carrying provisions for the one-year-long journey. Guided by a grand, unusual light in the sky, they were preoccupied with things heavenly—both celestial and prophetic.

All we really know is that they came, they asked around, they brought gifts, and they fell on their royal knees and faces to worship the baby God-in-the-straw.

What counts in this story is the complete unlikeliness of the circumstances, the setting, the key players, and the guest list. It does not make sense, and that's just as it should be. The recorded account of this event serves as a mere outline. In and of itself the gospel accounts barely suggest that the event of God becoming human flesh and walking among us may be the single most important moment in the human story.

The Tour

From this unlikely, ancient evening, my family came to commemorate those events by putting out, each Thanksgiving, just the little wooden manger and one lone cow.

In the weeks that followed, guests to our home would remark on the empty, incompleteness of the scene. "Oh, just putting out your Nativity."

"Nope," we'd say, "it's been there since Thanksgiving, but no one has arrived yet." At this point the visitor was either confused and would take on the worried look and cocked head of the family dog, or they'd "get it," smile (or just as often chuckle knowingly), and say, "But where's everybody else from the Nativity?"

We begin in our kitchen, homey and simple. There Mary and Joseph and the legendary donkey are to be found on the window sill over the sink—a common place, a family place. "Mary and Joseph arrived on the night before Christmas, so we move them to the manger in the entry hall on Christmas Eve night."

Then, we go upstairs to see the shepherds "in the hills" on the encyclopedia bookshelves, keeping watch. "They will arrive on Christmas night."

I always quietly relished the notion of simple shepherds hanging out on top of great, bulging volumes of the overly verbose *Encyclopaedia Britannica*.

"Back here," we explain, leading our tour to the eastern-most room of the house, "are the wise men. They will make the longest journey. They don't show up for a while. We place them in the manger on Epiphany, the day of the kings,

January 6." (Two days earlier and they might have gotten a piece of my birthday cake, too.)

At this point, our guest inevitably asks, "When do you put Jesus in the manger?" When I was giving the tour I was always tempted (and often succumbed) to say "November 15, 5 A.D." ever since I heard some youth pastor, halfway through his overly esoteric seminary training, spend an entire Sunday school hour telling us when Jesus was actually or more probably born, and then closing the hour by saying, "But what's important here is that we remember what Christmas is about, no matter when it really occurred." (He must have been a recovering fundamentalist trying to get "it" right.)

Eventually we'd tell our guest about "hiding" the Baby Jesus. "It must be hidden in plain sight—not behind the organ or under a sofa pillow or in a kitchen drawer amongst the corn-on-the-cob holders." The "plain sight" site must always be in the living room, dining room, or kitchen. (We didn't want to spend all Christmas morning looking for a 2"x3" statuette in the jam-packed garage.) The person who finds Jesus first says nothing, but just gloats while she or he moves on to the sofa and announces, "I found it." (No pun intended.) Then they wait for an appropriate moment to signal, with sly grin or leering eyes, to the "hider" that they indeed know where Jesus is hidden. The two of them wait and are vastly entertained while the rest of the clan try to find Him. (Even though our family was just four, we always had visitors — and not just for the holy days. There were a series of live-in guests for months or years at a time. In one case, for an entire decade and in two different houses.)

Whoever finds the "Christmas Kid" first is privileged to hide Him next year. That person has the additional distinction of acting as "Santa Claus" this year and distributing the gifts from under the tree.

Our family spent more than thirty-some Christmases together hiding Jesus and sending the shepherds upstairs to hang out with the *Britannica*. For a while I thought that when we get to Heaven, we wouldn't meet Jesus right away. In fact, we would be startled by how many folks there that we mistake for Jesus. He's hiding in plain sight. He blends in, belongs among us, just as God came to live among us, and has never really left. These days, though, Jesus is the one who passes out the gifts.

(Note: When I wrote the first draft of this story I shared it with my mother. She read these words—and several other chapters—and produced an article she had written about our family Christmas traditions. It had been published, back in 1967, in *Christian Teacher* magazine for instructors in private, church-related schools. Our memories of those traditions are not exactly the same, she told me. "But your book will not be about what we actually did. Rather it is about your memories of those times and how they affected you. Don't change a word." I have not changed substantive phrases since that conversation. You should know that my mother died of cancer in July of 1992. Our family Nativity scene is now in my care. Every year the shepherds, wise men, and Mary and Joseph show up in their assigned places.)

Our family's annual restaging of the Nativity was not the only Christmas tradition kept at Chez Wilson, though it was certainly the most unusual and dynamic. My mother made a series of decorations — mostly flower arrangements — themed to the metaphorical names given to Jesus in the Bible: Rose of Sharon, Lily of the Valley, etc. One of her favorites — and just about everyone else's — was the "Bright and Morning Star." She began making her sixteen-point

"Swedish Stars" in late summer. Each star was folded from shiny ribbon—all the same color, but a different color each year. She made new stars (one hundred of 'em) every year. Each star hung by a thread from the branches of an old manzanita tree. The tree, in turn, was hung from the ceiling with care. It appeared to be floating. It was—other than the Nativity—the single most talked about Christmas decoration in our house. Explaining its meaning drew attention to the other symbolic decorations around our house.

Dec the Halls, Every Room, the Stairs, Front Door . . .

All these meaning-filled decorations began in the early years of my parents' marriage. They lived in the wee town of Le Seuer, Minnesota (home, too, of the Jolly Green Giant). They taught in the local public high school and hosted many a social event in their home. This was their way of gently, but clearly, sharing their faith with any and all who came to party, bridge game, or social call.

In addition to the Nativity and the "names of Jesus flower arrangements," we had Christmas trees. That's right, trees as in more than one, at least two, sometimes three, and, one year, five. If there is to be only one Christmas a year, my folks decided early on, then it will last the whole season long and throughout the house. For us, that meant from just after Thanksgiving through and past Epiphany—January 6. That's why there has always been a Christmas tree around on my birthday—the fourth day of the year.

Our main (largest) Christmas tree was always in the living room, the least used room in our home. We never had a television there. The height of our main Christmas tree was always determined by the height of the ceiling, minus

an inch or two. One year, the height of the ceiling was determined by the tree, when we poked a hole in the living
room ceiling as we stood the tree up. That ceiling was that
awful "cottage-cheese-from-the-moon" stuff, so along with
poking a hole it snowed on the tree and the living room
carpet—a winter wonderland. My brother and I suggested
we add hole poking and ceiling snow to the list of annual
family traditions. We even tried to find a Bible verse to support it, inasmuch as we had seen the Holy Scriptures used
to support some pretty wild human notions. (No such verse
being found, our suggestion died in committee.) It should
come as no surprise to anyone that we decorated our trees
thematically as well. The main elements of the largest tree
were life-size white doves recalling the metaphor of God
as Holy Spirit descended upon Jesus as John baptized him.
To the doves were added hanging glass crystals (rescued
from some long forgotten chandelier), enormous clear plas-
tic snowflakes and large bows made from four-inch-wide
velvet ribbon. The bows were a different color every year,
but always just one color each year: cranberry, royal blue,
burgundy, red, and so on. We also had tiny white lights
throughout the tree and a dove, at the top, with wings
spread wide as if it had just settled in from flight. We never
could find an angel willing to sit for six weeks on top of
our tree. We didn't search very hard. Angels were probably
all in choir practice preparing for their upcoming appearance to the shepherds keeping watch over the encyclopedias
by night.

5

In the Middle of a Cold, Unfriendly, Winter's Night

Another winter's tale

> Without our traditions, our lives would be as crazy as a fiddler on the roof. —Tevye, philosopher and milkman

As the little town of Bethlehem found out, in the middle of a cold, unfriendly, winter's night, you never know who might show up.

One year, after my brother, Todd, was married and away, I had returned home to live with my folks to use them as home base while traveling extensively with my one-man play, *The Fifth Gospel* (about one hundred performances a year). We had a house filled with relatives and friends in from various corners of the map. We had just finished Christmas eve dinner and dessert and were starting the annual Yule jigsaw puzzle and board game tourney. Over the years we had cheated each other (uncles and aunts, brothers, sisters, and cousins) at everything from Pit, Risk, and Monopoly, to Clue, Shoots 'n' Ladders, Twister, and Rook. On my dad's side of the family, Rook was a full-contact sport. No high-stakes poker game in Vegas was as contentious as the Wilson Boys (my dad and his brothers) and their progeny playing Rook—a.k.a. Baptist Bridge, Protestant poker. (But "we don't play cards.") The innocent, the kind, the fainthearted need not apply. It was as much a spectator sport as pro wrestling or college basketball. (From the forthcoming tome, *We Might Cheat at Rook, But We Don't Gamble.*)

An Unexpected Call

In the midst of all this Protestant merrymaking, the telephone rang. Everyone immediately began guessing which missing relatives it might be, calling from Minneapolis, Potomac, Maryland, or Tacoma. Whoever answered the phone shouted for me. I grabbed the receiver to hear the voice of an old friend from Minneapolis. He and his wife were traveling around the country. They had made it halfway between L.A. and San Diego and wanted a recommendation for cheap lodgings for the night. His wife, though, was feeling sick. She was pregnant. That settled it: a young couple, on the road, away from home, Christmas Eve, sick and *with child.* There were three of them, my friend, his wife, and their young daughter.

"You're staying with us!" I announced.

No argument and no discussion. Even though we already had a full house, I did not need to ask my mom. Our family home was always ready for any and all travelers — year 'round — and they could stay as long as they needed to. My friend was an actor, not a carpenter, and with one child already in hand, there was nothing immaculate about the conception (even though my friend did graduate from Wheaton College, boot camp for the army of God). Besides, with a house full of church folk, we weren't about to turn away a traveling pregnant couple on Christmas Eve. A situation like this could go two ways: turning them away could mean major cosmic demerits, and bringing them in was at least a sermon illustration — or a good story in a book someday.

They arrived about forty minutes later, which gave us time to decide where to comfortably house them. They were to have my room: a good-sized bed for my friend and his wife, sleeping bag for their daughter—who arrived asleep—and easy access to a bathroom. I was to sleep on the big and comfortable family room couch with blankets, pillows, big TV, cable, and remote control. I vividly remember lying there thinking about that first Christmas Eve and another jam-packed Inn on a holiday weekend. Was it absolutely full? Was there really not one room or an old blanket thrown on the floor near the cooking fire? Was there no couch in the lobby or had that too been leased for the night? Was there just a "No Pregnant Guests" policy in force that night?

My friends—Sandy and Rich Allison and their daughter, Inga — slept through the night. Sandy felt much better in the morning. Their baby was not born during the night, but over the years we have stayed in touch and whenever we see each other, we almost always talk about the Christmas of 1980. She always asks if my mom still does the Nativity step-by-step and the names of Jesus flower arrangements.

"Yup. Every year," I tell her, "and Mary and Joseph don't go into the manger until late on Christmas Eve. Just like you did. Just in time!"

6

My Parents Were Professional Christians
The Gospel According to My Mom and Dad

Honor your father and your mother
that you may live long on the earth.
—Fourth Commandment, Exodus 20:12

We were just back from a weekend of church camp—I was twelve years old—and our senior minister was interviewing me during the Sunday night service at church.

Pastor Joe began, "Did you have a good weekend at camp?"

"Yes, sir, we had a fantastic weekend!"

"Aren't both of your parents in full-time Christian service?" He asked.

"They're both professional Christians," I answered before even thinking about what I had said. That off-handed comment elicited a good deal of laughter and became a phrase that I have used ever since when speaking about my mom and dad. As the laughter subsided, the pastor tried to recover his composure and make some sense of my comment.

"You mean they're in full-time Christian service?"

"Well, their jobs are also a ministry, so I call 'em professional Christians."

"Professional Christians. What are their jobs?"

"You know, my mom is the speech therapist and drama teacher at the school here."

"San Gabriel Christian School, here at our church."

"Right, and my dad's the principal."

"Your dad's the principal."

"He's also the guy who sits behind you on the platform on Sunday mornings while you're preaching, and when your sermon is too long, he pulls your microphone cord to haul you back over to the pulpit."

"So that's what all those yanks are about."

Dad on a Pedestal

To say that my dad was a hero in my mind doesn't begin to cover the matter. I never believed my dad walked on water, but he did swim several laps of the swimming pool in our backyard every morning—rain or shine.

"Bracing!" He'd exclaim as he came in from the cold of a Northern California winter, steam rolling off him like a fresh-braised Christmas goose.

Such was the verve and élan with which he attacked most everything in his life. His faith was no exception. In fact, his faith was at the core of who he was, and it was the most clearly observable part of his character. He was, quite simply, the most Christ-like person I have ever known.

Like Jesus, my dad was a teacher whose primary tools were story and inquiry. He was warm-fire-in-the-hearth friendly and endlessly engaging without needing to be the center of attention. Everyone liked him—everyone. His quick wit could be just the trick to ease tensions or re-ignite a dull moment. More than any other characteristic, I admired his gentle strength. He put up with a lot and rarely chose to fight fire with fire, though at six feet tall and 210 pounds he had plenty of fire available. He was the most patient creature I ever encountered, and unfailingly trustworthy.

At my dad's memorial service, in 1992, Glen Anderson said, "Every pastor needs an Elwood Wilson—a man to be his friend and confidant who he can trust and go to with anything. It was my privilege to be Wils's pastor in San Jose and in San Diego. I am twice blessed."

He could be tough, whether he was going out late at night to track down a church friend at a motel and rescue him from an extramarital affair (dragging him to Denny's for an order of tough love and black coffee), or standing against a small army of parents determined to tell him how to run his school.

I do not have all his patience, but aspire every day to be more like him in that regard. Whenever my emotional teapot is about to whistle, I try to catch myself and ask, "Okay, what would your old dad say?" It is surprisingly effective in turning down the heat. Mostly, he knew how to put life in perspective.

Axiomatic Parenting

My dad could teach more with a question or a turned phrase than anyone I have ever encountered. Go to him with a vexing problem that, in the moment, seemed insurmountable and could be solved only with his direct involvement, and he'd say, "Sounds like a personal problem to me."

On the surface, this seemed heartless, uncaring, and, at the very least, unhelpful. But early on he would explain to my brother and me that he wanted us to take the situation in hand — our hands. He believed we could do something about the matter, that we were not as helpless as we imagined ourselves to be, even as young boys.

He would always follow up with the very empowering, "What are you going to do about it?"

If I said, "I don't know. That's why I'm asking you," he'd ask, "What do you think?"

"I DON'T KNOW!"

My frustration did not motivate him to jump in and solve my problem.

"You must know *something.* Tell me what you *do* know." Then he'd talk me through a line of inquiry that almost always led to a plan, a solution. Eventually I didn't run to him, or my mom, with every little pothole on the road of childhood. In school, in conversations with peers, it became clear to both my brother and me that this solve-our-own-problems approach was not universally practiced in every family. I don't remember even a few friends whose parents let them make *all* their own decisions.

My parents even believed that my brother and I should have the final say when it came to which schools we'd attend.

The only time that I regretted choosing to stay in private church-related schools was the year we moved to Northern California and lived in the resort community of Mount Hermon. The local public high school was small, close, and had art, drama, and tackle football. My brother and I opted for the church-related school that was over the mountains, down in the Santa Clara Valley. (See *Climb Every Mountain.*) Then, one night our whole family went to see the school play at the little public high school near us. It was a glorious, charming, and thoughtful production of Thorton Wilder's *Our Town.* Darn! I most probably would have been in that production. Meanwhile, plays at the church-related school were sappy Christmas pageants ("Jesus and the Indians Go to Bethlehem") directed by some mom who took a drama class in college.

Quotations from Chairman Elwood

My dad's creative teaching and parenting most often took the form of aphorism or homily.

"All of life is Plan B," my dad used to say. This was neither a statement of pessimism nor resignation. He was a planner, an anticipator, an action taker. He would more often ask "what if" than "what," and he usually asked "What're you up to" instead of "How are you?" Understanding life as plan "B" was a way of getting ready for the rest of the day, the rest of life. He taught me to play chess six, ten, twelve moves in advance.

The person with a backup plan—"Plan B"—would be the person most likely to prepared for anything.

He would often say, "If the only way folks know that you're a Christian is by what you say, then you only have Christian lips." That one was a personal favorite of mine.

If I messed up on a project, he might offer the heartfelt: "What'd you do that for?" He really wanted to know the thinking that had led to such a result.

Delightfully enough, he was more engaged by an earnest and valiant effort that produced a weak result than a half-hearted, timid effort that led to a good result. "Try it!" he'd say about anything new or unfamiliar, often followed by, "You might like it." Thus my discovery of foods that have been known to gag lesser mortals, such as: pickled herring, horseradish, and smoked oysters. He'd toss you into the deep end of any circumstance rather than let you learn a small lesson in the shallow end of life.

On any of the numerous occasions when my brother and I fought over nothing, my dad, hearing the pounding on the floor becoming more rigorous, would come to the foot of the stairs and yell up to us, "Don't make me come up there!" Our hearts quickened as we considered settling the matter rather than facing the addition of an enormous former All-American footballer into our sniveling little sibling skirmish.

Years later, we shared our lifelong fear about those threats.

"Threat?" He was amazed that we had added that meaning to what he intended as "encouragement." "I wanted you two to work it out on your own, and I knew you could do that without the fighting. I never came up there and settled your battles. You did it—every time."

To this day, more than a decade after his passing, whenever I come to a major decision in life, I imagine the sort of questions he'd ask me whenever I sought his counsel. It still works.

What Are You Drinking?

Perhaps the best example of my dad's unwavering belief in people was a simple incident. It had happened hundreds of times in my life.

I was visiting my mom and dad for the evening — they lived about forty minutes from me in the Los Angeles area. As we were preparing to sit down to dinner, my dad stood in front of the refrigerator, holding the door open. He asked me, "What are you drinking? Milk, ice tea, Coke, juice, water. . . ."

I was baffled. I went over to him and looked right at him. "You've known me all my life. Why do you ask me that?

When have you seen me drink anything other than water or milk at dinner?"

Without skipping a beat my dad said, "A person can change." (I was in my late thirties.)

It sounds little, insignificant, but it was his essence.

My Mother and Other Women of the Bible

My parents were both enormously creative, although my mother was the artistic one. If you asked folks who knew her what kind of an artist she was, you might hear playwright, flower arranger, decorator, poet, musician, theatrical director, crafter, costumer, chef, illustrator, character actress, and a host of others. Every one of those was correct, and no one fit better than any other. She, in turn, had an enormously creative mother, and her oldest brother—my uncle Paul—was an artist and art educator.

Whatever you needed, she could "whip something up" in no time at all.

She could not recall or tell the simplest joke to save her life, but could recount an incident from her day and portray all the characters with hilarious specificity.

Late in life — in her early sixties — she applied for and got a job at the big high school in her area as a tutor, teacher's aide, and factotum. She would come home and re-enact her day, which included students and staff of numerous ethnic dialects and sensibilities. She never ridiculed them, but honored their uniqueness and individuality — albeit farcically.

My mom had a mastery for making the most ordinary moments in life an occasion. During our elementary school years, she would pick us up from school many afternoons. Every other Thursday was "Shopping Day." My dad had school board and church board meetings those evenings, and my mother would take my brother and me shopping and then out for dinner. We got to buy something — a toy, game, new "bike bag" (the canvas forerunner of the modern-day student backpack). Todd and I so looked forward to "Shopping Day" that it often transformed a tough week into a much happier one. Rain or shine, we went shopping and out for dinner, two Thursdays each month for years.

As clever and jump-in-with-both-feet helpful as my mom was, she could also stop, sit, and listen intensely to the most urgent matter in our lives.

Even then she was artistic. "Let's discuss this over a cup of tea." I didn't drink tea as a kid, my brother didn't, and neither did my mom, but that didn't stop her from pouring cold milk into one of her beautiful tea cups and loading a plate with cookies and retiring to the formal living room to sit and have "tea and cakes" while we settled the world's problems. During winter months cold milk was replaced by hot chocolate—her own special recipe.

She was also an avid student of the Bible, focusing much of her study on the scores of women God has used throughout both the Old and New Testament to serve and fulfill the Creator's plan.

My mother was such a go-getter that I suspect she invented the philosophy "easier to get forgiveness later than permission in advance." Had she waited for permission she might have accomplished only half of all she did and spent a lot more time sitting around—something she never did.

From my mother, I learned a deep appreciation for worship, though most of the churches I grew up in had a flimsy sense of worship. Ask your garden variety churchgoer coming out of the standard All-American-Evangelical Sunday morning gather of Churchianity, "How was worship today?" They will likely respond, "The sermon was good." Or, "The pastor was good today."

As my mother would say, "Evangelicals don't do worship. They have preaching with a pre-show." If the preacher is no good, there is no worship, so they believe. But there is more to worship than a forty-five-minute Hebrew lesson.

My mother was raised Episcopalian. Early on she exposed my brother and me to liturgical worship by taking us to both Episcopal and Roman Catholic services on occasion. Like my dad, she was not afraid to expose my brother and me to a variety of life options, discuss them in detail, and leave us with the final choice. My parents received no small amount of criticism for the wide berth of individual freedom they gave my brother and me.

"Women should be silent in church" (1 Cor. 8:69)

My mother's pursuit of her goals and dreams was so complete that when the "women's movement" came into focus in the sixties I didn't get it at first. Sure there are obstacles to achieving personal and professional goals. You go around them, change them, or follow Michelangelo's advice: "Creativity is the best revenge."

There were so many projects, opportunities, and pursuits that I had witnessed my mom go after and achieve that I honestly could not make sense of the virulent fight for equality of the sexes in the marketplace. When I finally asked my mom about "women's lib" she smiled and said, "Some people need a movement to energize them or a team to support them. I always had my parents cheering me on, and your dad is my biggest fan."

My mom and dad were my fans, my coaches, my champions for all of my dreams — even the ones they didn't understand. Even the ones I didn't understand.

In the Academy Award–winning film *Chariots of Fire,* British runner Eric Little is confronted by his sister about his choice to try out for the Olympic track team rather than returning with the family to continue their missionary work in China.

"I know the Lord made me a good preacher, but He also made me fast, and when I run I feel His pleasure."

To this day, I feel my mother and father's pleasure when I tenaciously and dauntlessly pursue life. Even when I fail, I hear my dad say, "What do you want to do?"

7

The French Toast
That Changed My Life
Not a wasted weekend

God has no grandchildren.
—Louis Palau

Thicker than your hand and sweeter than angel food cake, it was the best French toast in the whole wide world. At least that's what I told my mom and dad after my first weekend camp away from home. The place was Green Oaks Boys Ranch in Vista, California. (Today it is Green Oaks Boys *and* *Girls* Ranch—a sign of the "end times.") My brother and I were fascinated by their seemingly endless resourcefulness.

"...and they raise their own ham and eggs!" We thought this was cool that on tour of camp we could meet chickens and pigs that might well be providing our breakfast the next morning. The pigs might *be* breakfast.

Green Oaks was owned and operated by the Union Rescue Mission of Los Angeles. Back then, they actually had an enormous neon sign on the roof of the building proclaiming: JESUS SAVES. As a result of their work with the homeless in the streets of L.A., many camp workers were men recovering from various addictions and other difficulties.

One such fellow had been a successful chef in famous restaurants in his day. These days, he cooked for fourth, fifth, and sixth grade boys — ages nine to eleven. But no wallpaper paste gruel served here. He baked his own bread, sliced it thicker than your head, and dipped it in his own "secret recipe" batter. The result was French toast better than I have tasted before or since!

After my third trip to Green Oaks and endless ravings, my mom visited camp to interrogate the chef as to the secret of his batter. "I divide the yokes from the egg white and whip them separately before recombining them and adding cinnamon and nutmeg." The Truth was now known. Henceforth, my mother would purchase bread from a bakery, slice it thick as our heads, and dip it languidly in a batter of separated eggs. Harmony and tranquility were at last restored to our family breakfasts.

On that first trip to Green Oaks Ranch, I was ten years old. An entire busfull of boys and men from our church headed off for a full weekend. This was church camp. A weekend filled with singing, storytelling, sleeping bags, hiking, and scripture reading. Just men and boys, and Jesus.

I knew all about Jesus. I'd been going to Sunday school all my life (save one particular Sunday) and had heard or read every major event in the Gospel story several times over, so I wasn't expecting much in the way of religious revelation at Green Oaks.

The days were rich and full, and the nights were all campfires and stars. But this weekend, it rained Saturday night. Campfire was moved indoors to a big hall with an enormous fireplace. That night as the speaker told the story of Jesus' death on the cross, I was distracted by the thought of all those grown men who had given up a weekend from their families to be with a bunch of squirrely boys. Why would they do that? I knew all of these men and their families. What were they getting out of being away for three days?

Then the speaker said it. A short, simple observation that would literally change my life. Quoting a popular evangelist, the camp speaker said, "Louis Palau once observed that *'God has no grandchildren.'*"

Got it. Being a child of God is about joining a one generation family. Entering that family was a choice—my choice. Just as I knew I was the eldest son of Donna and Elwood Wilson, I now realized that to be a child of God I had to take that step on my own. I had to embrace Jesus' sacrifice on the cross for me. That my parents and grandparents had each done this did not cover me. It wasn't like being on my dad's insurance policy.

For me, becoming a Christian was knowing that I am not able to live my life without God's help. Being in touch with my Creator completes me. Christ's sacrifice for me on the cross makes me whole. My sin, my selfishness, gets in the way of pursuing God's grand design for my life.

I know all that now, some forty years later. At the time, I knew that men in my church, who I liked and respected, gave up a weekend to be with a scraggly, distracted, rambunctious herd of young colts on a little ranch in one corner of God's garden. They had all become God's children and wanted us to join the family. I knew they wouldn't waste their weekend on kids unless there was a good reason. If these men believed in God and loved Jesus enough to hang out with us, that made a powerful and meaningful impression on me.

That night I asked Jesus to be in my life, through his Holy Spirit. That night I chose to be my Creator's child. I was ten. It was not a wasted weekend.

Sometimes God works in miraculous and mysterious ways to demonstrate the eternal love and abundant life available to us. Sometimes our Creator needs only a rainy night with a bunch of guys gathered in front of a big fireplace and an ample supply of the best darn French toast on earth.

8

Just One Sunday

A very important morning

RICK: I came to Casablanca for the waters.

LOUIE: The waters. What waters? We're in the desert.

RICK: I was misinformed.

—Humphrey Bogart (Rick), Claude Raines (Louie)
in *Casablanca*

When you go to church every Sunday, every year, all of your life, it is part of who you are — like brushing your teeth. You don't think about not doing it any more than you would consider not going to regular school Monday through Friday, September through June. It's what you do.

Then one Sunday I considered not going to church. I had thought about not going many times. This Sunday would be different. This Sunday I would not just think about it; I would say something. It is one of the most powerful, life-changing memories I have — one of the most important events of my childhood. I think about it all the time. It is the day that my whole family learned about a deep part of who I am to this day. On this Sunday I learned what going to church meant for me. More importantly I learned about what faith is for me, personal.

The Human Alarm Clock

Sunday morning always got started with my dad getting up very early. As I think about it, every day of my childhood started with my dad getting up early. Back then, he was in charge of waking everyone in his time zone. As a kid I totally believed that. Now, well, I know better—he was only in charge of waking up Southern California. He'd make the rounds of our house with his characteristic high-pitched whistle and near-legendary, "Rise 'n' Shine" (a greeting in the form of a bark that he'd acquired from the United States Navy).

"Rise 'n' shine" was always followed by, "Time to get up" and often the German greeting "A rowse ma ting!" (Even though we were direct descendants of Frederick I, Emperor of Germany, we had stopped speaking German on a daily basis when the family arrived on the shores of the New World in about 1760. "A rowse ma ting!" was the lone remnant of that pedigree.) Nonetheless, that is how our days began, six days each week. There was a second whistle and then a final (for now) "Get up." On Sundays the phrase "Time to get ready for church" supplanted "get up."

My brother and I would roll over, groan, growl, and mumble, "Isstoowurrrly" (*sic*) and go back to sleep. At least we headed back for sleep. We rarely got all the way back. Our dad came back—always—two or three trips. There'd be more whistling, more Navy cheers, more German, and often a toe tug or flying pillow—"Incoming!"

I was ten years old and in fifth grade when it happened. As my dad made his rounds this particular Sunday morning I groaned from my cotton cocoon, "I don't wanna go to church today." He didn't much notice till he whistled through a few minutes later and asked, "Are you getting up for church today?" His tone suggested that I actually had the option not to get up for church. I knew better, but took a chance that I might actually have a choice in the matter.

"No." Resolute, not defiant.

Then he engaged, "You're not going to church?"

"No, I'm not going," I reiterated.

Then he asked the Big Question. It was one of those questions you get asked every few years and the rest of your life rests on your answer. You know that if you do not get it exactly right, God will strike you blind or hit you in the arm with lightning and the mark will never go away, so the rest of your life all will know you got one of the Big Questions wrong. This was such a moment.

"Not going?"

"No, I'm not going today," reiterating my reiteration.

Then the Big Question. "Are you sick?" Bum, ba, bum, bum! (Dragnet theme). And the universe held its breath in anticipation of my answer.

I was not sick, but if I said I wasn't sick I would have to go to church because being sick was the only excuse any kid had ever heard of for not going to church — except being dead. (Even then, you'd still have to dress up and lie there while everybody funeralized you without opportunity for rebuttal.)

Before I answered the Big Question ("Are you sick?") I thought, I've been going to church fifty-two weeks every year for the past ten years — the *only* ten years I'd ever had. (The only Sundays I had missed were to attend church camp and up there we had four church meetings in three days.) Couldn't I not go just this once and just because I didn't want to? Hadn't I earned a few free Sundays on my "Frequent Faithful" account? I had no special reason; I just didn't want to go. Period.

I thought all of this in the moment between the Big Question and my little answer.

Moreover, I could not lie to get out of going to church. That would be immediate, irrevocable, nontransferable, everybody-would-know-about-it-cuz-you'd-have-to-wear-a-big-sign Cosmic Demerits.

I held my breath and blurted out, *"No!* I'm not sick."

"Okay," my dad said and turned to leave my bedroom.

"Wait a minute." Calling him back into the room I asked another Big(ish) question, "What do you mean, 'Okay'?"

"Okay, you're not sick," he said, as casually as if he were telling me the time. "If you were sick I'd get something to make you more comfortable, soothing, while we're at church." Again he left.

"So-o-o-o!" Summoning him back, "am I (gulp) going?"

Re-entering, "Do you want to go?"

"No."

"All right."

"All right what?" I needed to know.

"All right, you're not going to church."

"Because—?" I wanted to know exactly why.

"Because you don't want to go today." He left my room.

I was ticked! It was just too darn easy not to go to church. All those Sundays, all those years, that I'd been whistled awake and went to church because I thought there was no choice. No options. Church is where God lives, and not to go would be to refuse an invitation to visit God in his house.

Then with one gentle and simple shrug my dad reminded me, taught me, that if I went to church it was for the best of all possible reasons: I wanted to go. It was not because he made me go—as his parents made him go—and there would be no discussion about it. I went to church because I like it and chose to go. I like all my friends that I went to Sunday school with and all the adults that were my friends as well as my parents' friends. I liked the great old hymns, mostly, and the big loud organ Ivan Baker played so enthusiastically and so artistically with both hands and both feets. I liked drawing in church. (See more of my church doodles in "Drawing in Church," chapter 13.) I especially like watching my dad sitting on the platform. When Pastor Joe got his new Lavaliere mic, so he could come out from behind the big wooden monument to the National Lumberjack Hall of Fame, it was my dad's job to manage the long microphone cord. (This was before wireless mics.) When Pastor Joe walked way over to the far side of the stage—toward the Europe and Asia half of the lighted missionary map, my dad gave him lots of cord. When Pastor Joe returned to the pulpit my dad would reel him in like a deep sea fisherman who had bagged a 180-pound southern preacher.

All of a sudden, an otherwise normal Sunday morning, and a single gesture, transformed my world forever. There'd be no long microphone cord or cartoons in church, nor anxious and endless waiting after church to go to lunch at Gus's Pit Bar-B-Q. None of that this week. I was not going to church because I didn't want to go.

It is one of the most vivid experiences of my youth, and do you know what I did? I can't remember. I haven't a whiff of memory about what I did all those hours at home, alone. Probably turned on every TV, banged on the baby grand, and enjoyed a continuous breakfast.

It's a good guess I tried to watch some religious TV — just in case. In those days, unfortunately, my choices would have been bleak: an Oral Roberts tent meeting and healing service, Rex Humbard, and their ilk. Most probably I leaped from the sofa and turned the dial to Los Angeles channel 9 to watch the "Million Dollar Movie." It would have been a classic from the forties or before. I probably watched it twice.

What I do remember is that the next Sunday I went back to church. I've been going every Sunday ever since because I love it—now more than ever. Every time I sit there, I know I'm there because I want to be there.

Besides, church is God's house and there is this big old cookie jar there—like at my gramma's house. The difference is that God lets you take the jar home with you and it's filled with something better than cookies. It's filled with Grace. My dad reached in there one Sunday morning and gave me a big helping—delicious!

> "And the truth shall set you free."
> (Even if you're only ten years old)

9

Lutheran Sex

We were just looking

I'll tell you a great secret, my friend. Don't wait for the
last judgment. It happens every day.   —Albert Camus

If they didn't want us kissing on campus, they should have
told us right up front. Nothing was said. Not a word. Since
this was my first time attending a private school, and they
knew that, I would've expected them to be very clear about
outlining Lutheran behavior, especially Lutheran sex. But
I wasn't a Lutheran when I came to Lutheran Academy. I
wasn't much of anything. I was five years old, a kinder-
gartner. I was at the beginning of everything.

I honestly did not know on the first day that my sex
life would begin there as well. That is, if you consider a
five-year-old's deliberately planted kiss on the mouth "sex."
At the age of five it was plenty sexual for my onlooking,
completely surprised, and totally shocked classmates.

Years later, I would realize that my sex life had actually begun earlier during preschool, in the garage of our
family home back in Le Seuer, Minnesota. We played "doctor." Didn't everyone? Maybe not at age four, but you
must have peeked at a friend's anatomy during your de-
velopmental years. Didn't we all wonder? Maybe that's
why they're called the "wonder" years. My wonder years

included a Monday through Friday fascination with An-
nette Funicello's ever-expanding Mouseketeer sweater. Her
name seemed to get longer and longer.

Garage Memorial

My first "practice" as a doctor was with the little girls in my
neighborhood. Some came for weekly—even twice weekly—
checkups. That's all they ever were, just checkups...check-
downs, check-all-arounds, and check-one-more-time. At
every "appointment" we checked just about everything,
again. When we were done checking, we were done. Checking is all we knew how to do. It all started fairly innocently. I
don't believe we had any idea how revelatory it would be—
especially the first major discovery of the primary sexual
difference between boys and girls.

Certainly that was a surprise, but it was not frightening.
My "patients" were only girls. Having a brother with whom
I shared tub, bedroom, and underwear drawer made the
need for boy patients unnecessary. There was no wonder
for me there. Now, lest you think I was a strict patrician
in the classic 1950s *Father Knows Best* tradition, you should
know that I was not always cast in the role of doctor. We
took turns, the girls and I, peeking about torso-land. I'm
not sure, thinking back on it all, which role I enjoyed the
most: peeker or peekee, checker or checkee.

The garage of our family home was our clinic. It was
there that the Mom and Dad Bunko Squad busted up our
little family practice. We were in mid-exam when—without
warning — my mom came into the garage unannounced.
Surprisingly enough, she did not act surprised. She wasn't—
as I recall—angry, either. My punishment was to sit down

with my mom and dad and tell them what we had been doing, for how long, and why. I'm sure, too, that they must have asked, "Was it fun?" "Did you enjoy it?" Knowing the way my folks handled discipline through the years I'm sure they must've asked me if I had any questions. I'm sure I did, and that I did not ask any at the time. I would have to wait another three long years—second grade—before I learned of the relationship between "tab A" and "slot B." Those are the very words used by the kid who first described male/female intercourse to me. That was a new concept that I found puzzling, enlightening, and not—for the moment—an attraction.

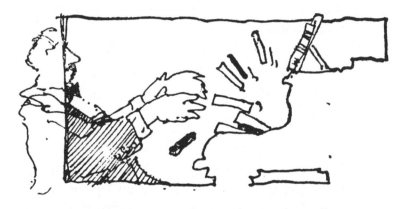

The whole form-follows-function nature of "A" into "B," though obvious, was not a part of the discussion. It was more a mystery — a wonder! I do remember thinking — as one of my chief and earliest thoughts on this whole intercourse thing — Does God know that people are...A- and B-ing? Must know. God created A and B. If God created "them (us) man and woman" in God's own image, then is God: A or B, both A and B, or none of the above? (er...below.) Eventually God's A-ness and/or B-ness didn't matter, either.

What mattered was that at age four I was poking around the bodies of my female playmates, my folks caught us at it, and I was not punished. I was strongly urged never to do it again.

I stopped—for several years.

Meanwhile, back at the young Lutherans' compound, the school year was in full flower. Often we were all together at our desks or seated around the rug with our chairs in a circle. Such occasions were for "show and tell," story time or special visits from Mr. Fireman, Mr. Policeman, or Pastor "Shirt-on-Backwards," as I came to call the clerical-collared Lutheran minister.

It was just after a circle time that, as we were all chatting and giggling, I got up out of my chair, went over to one of the girls in my class, and kissed her, square on the mouth. I was immediately reprimanded, not for kissing, but for getting out of my seat. (Since then I have learned to kiss in a seated position.)

This was, after all, my very first real kiss. To be honest, even though that kiss was thrilling — on a five-year-old's scale of emotions—I am certain that I was motivated more by the theatricality of the moment than by the sexuality. That first kiss was such a big surprise that it triggered several years of celibacy.

Four Years Later

The next kiss was in fourth grade. This one was sexual, both in intent and experience. I was nine and she was a championship roller skater named Debbie. She had sequined outfits with very short skirts, matching panties and shoe covers, and lots of freckles. That was when I first discovered my attraction to women with freckles—I am still drawn, like moth to flame, to a woman with freckles. Don't ask, I can't explain it, and don't want to. The roller rink where she practiced was just two blocks from our school, so I would walk down and watch. My dad picked me up when his day was done, since he was the principal at the church school I attended from third through eighth grade. Debbie got a ride from her mom. Everybody knew we were boyfriend and girlfriend. We passed notes in class. Duh! I even spent an entire geography lesson figuring out how to spell the sound of a kiss for a note on which I had drawn a large pair of lips. M-m-m-v-u-h! I handed it to her at the end of the day, a Friday. She loved it. She opened it, looked, smiled, and blushed so big that most of her freckles disappeared. The ensuing twinkle in her eye was the best feeling I had ever had in my whole life—up to that point. (All nine years.)

Not long after that, I was standing at the rail of the Shamrock Roller Rink in San Gabriel, California, watching Debbie do her final routine of the day. She finished splendidly, and sailed straight to me at full speed. If it hadn't been for the rail between us, we might have been touching from head to skates. I didn't move. I knew then that this was a key moment on its way to becoming a major memory.

"My mom wants to take us out for hamburgers," she smiled.

"Great! I'll call my dad and see if it's okay," I said, while inside a chorus of "Oh, boys!" were running around shouting, "A DATE!"

"I'll go change."

When she didn't move right away, but stood there as we smiled at each other, I leaned forward and planted a big kiss on her. Looking back, it may not have been that big a kiss, but, c'mon, we were only nine years old! Any kiss would have been a whopper. I'm sure her mom saw us. Somehow, that made the entire event even more exciting! It was absolutely a whole new life after that.

I have moments when I suddenly realize I'm starring in a movie of my life. It may be a thrilling, fearful encounter, great passion, or relief. It's seeing the Grand Canyon for the first time, or being called "Uncle" by my new, little, and finally talking niece. So, at the same time I'm leaning forward to kiss Debbie, I can feel the camera coming in for the Cinemascope close-up as the lush Elmer Bernstein score swells.

(CRANE SHOT. PULL BACK AND UP.)

(GIRL SPINS ON SKATES. GLIDES ACROSS RINK FLOOR, THROUGH POOLS OF LIGHT.)

(BOY TURNS, LEANS AGAINST RAILING. HEAD BACK. HE IS BEAMING.)

It was that kind of moment in my nine-year-old mind, when I was overtaken by an attack of puppy love. Heck, this was full-grown-dog-howling-at-the-moon love.

Her mom never mentioned the kiss to either of us. We did go out for a burger, and her mom let us sit at our own table. It was a date!

Most kids I grew up with would never have been allowed to go on even a chaperoned date at only nine years old. Doesn't matter that is was just for a burger and her mom was sitting within striking distance. Most kids weren't allowed to date for decades.

When I told my fourth grade friends about it later, they could not believe I had kissed her—and in front of her mom.

"My mom would have killed me," a shocked buddy responded.

He was right—I knew his mom.

10

Making Out in the Sixties
Never ask my mom about French kissing

Try to set the night on *fire*.
—The Doors

After moving to California, I never played doctor again. Well...not for a very long time, anyway.

Before I had ever heard the term, I had my first "French kiss." Either I had it early or my friends were keeping their mouths shut, so to speak, about this miraculous maneuver.

I didn't realize until years later, after talking with friends with a different background than mine, that I grew up with a group of sexual early bloomers and quick starters. By today's standards, we would be prudes, but in the 1960s, for sixth and seventh graders to be "making out" was a big deal. Remember "making out"?

The site of this historic event was a party in the basement family room at the home of a classmate. This was a girl-planned event, which meant there would be precisely the same number of girls and boys in attendance.

There were always "visiting adults" hanging out with the host parents at every party. The excuse was always, "Oh, they just stopped by for a while." Right! They were reinforcements, in case there was an outbreak of mud wrestling or a sudden and unexpected loosening of shirt buttons and

zippers and the subsequent loss of clothing. No such luck—
not even in my progressive seventh grade.

Eventually the games portion of the evening commenced:
"Honey, If You Love Me," "Orange-under-the-neck relay,"
life savers on a toothpick, and the age old, surefire classic
"Spin the Bottle." We still had pop bottles to spin back then,
and spin we did. A friend later confessed to me that prior to
this evening he had never before, in the dozen long years of
his life, kissed a girl on the mouth. On this particular candlelit evening, he kissed six different girls on their mouth.
I chose not to tell, let alone brag, of my previous lip-to-lip
encounters in kindergarten and fourth grade.

When Girls Plan a Party

The candles-only lighting for the evening was also the doing
of the all-girl planning committee.

"It's so romantic," quipped one of the guys sarcastically.

"It's so dark!" Added our resident dope.

Finally one of the girls settled it, "It's Ni-i-i-ce." Worked
for me. "Nice" is a very popular motif among church families. It's the adjective of choice for those not wanting to
stand out too much in the crowd. "Nice" is just a notch
above "good," not far from "okay" and ridiculously close
to "plain." Amongst church folk, "plain" is acceptable. It's
much preferable to "different," "flashy," "fashionable," or
"trendy." Sticking out is completely unacceptable. Drawing attention to one's self by any means—behavior, attire,
possessions—is not acceptable. "Nice" is best. Everyone in
the church jokes about what the Eleventh Commandment
might have been, but Commandment number 10 "b" was,
"Thou shalt be nice, all the time." Jesus restated it in the

Sermon on the Mount (Matthew 5), "Blessed are the nice, for they shall not attract attention unto themselves."

No one sticks out in the dark. The dark is at once the great equalizer and the great encourager. Darkness is scary, romantic (with candles), protective, comforting, and, in movies or on rainy nights, dangerous. In junior high school, I used the dark to be braver with girls. In the dark, I was handsome. I spoke slower and more quietly. In the dark you move more gently. That, too, is sexy or at least as sexy as a junior high boy and girl could get at a party of kids from a church-related school in the mid-1960s. The sexual revolution was being waged in Berkeley and Boulder and the Bohemian neighborhoods of New York City, but not in Southern California's San Gabriel Valley. There, middle-class American churchgoers took root, and twelve-year-old sexual explorers took their time — fearfully — in the dark, with candles all around the room and visiting adults in the kitchen.

I'm not sure where the term "making out" came from. Probably two teenage couples at the beach separated by a small sand dune. The two boys would take a break in the proceedings to run over the dune and ask, "How are you making out?" They weren't looking for instructions or tips, necessarily, just encouragement and a progress report.

My friends and I mostly watched each other that night, learning by example. Just as fathers don't stop and ask directions when they're lost, junior high boys don't ask girls how they like to be kissed. The room is dark, so visibility is limited. What the eye cannot see, the mind imagines. There we were: the blind leading the blundering. Not knowing what to do exactly, we didn't know if we were even doing it right, and so no one complained.

This we knew: "Don't take your clothes off and don't …ah… 'sleep' together!" What a dumb phrase: "Are you sleeping with anyone?" In Sunday school we learned about King David's rooftop view of Bathsheba, his neighbor lady, and her open air, moonlit hot tub. Eventually, they slept together. We imagined, too, there may have been a fair amount of "making out" before the "sleeping."

But no Sunday school teacher ever said that. We knew that this kind of "sleeping" was wrong. But, if you were married, "sleeping together" changed to "being fruitful and multiplying," and that was all right. In fact, it is encouraged—from on High. In junior high we slept alone.

In the middle and late 1960s, the church was so intent on discouraging us from doing "grass," dropping acid, and joining the free love movement that they skipped right over "making out." Now and then, an adult would elevate heavy petting to the stature of sin—right up there on the sin hit parade with lying, cheating, and sleeping together.

If heavy petting—usually defined as hands inside clothing other than your own and skin against skin—was a sin, you can imagine the overwhelming silence that the church has accorded masturbation. Almost nobody talked about it. Ever. Certainly it was never dealt with in church, Sunday school, or private school. It was a subject that the church would not "touch." Like most touchy subjects we learned about it from older friends and "famous parents." That was the mom who had not grown up in a church family and had lived a colorful life before joining the church. She was open-minded, colorful, and, some would say, a bad influence. Or we learned about sexual taboos from a famous father who had most certainly been in the Navy.

I learned from both my mom and my dad. My mother did grow up in a church family, but she, like her parents before her, was very open to discussing anything, which meant we discussed *everything*. The opposite was true of my dad's family. He'd been raised in a very strict, legalistic church family. His parents were quite devout. They had quite tender and playful sides, but Grampa and Gramma Wilson were not so open-minded or worldly-minded as Grampa and Gramma Beckman, my mother's parents, late of Corwith, Iowa. And my dad was in the Navy!

Grampa Wilson Meets Raquel Welch

Grampa Wilson was not without great character, however. My Uncle Roy, one of my father's two older brothers, brought Grampa with him on one of his many visits to my apartment when I attended college in Minneapolis. By then, Grampa and Gramma Wilson were living in a retirement home just a couple of miles from my apartment. One of my roommates had acquired a life-size poster of Raquel Welch in a bikini top and a pair of tight fitting jeans. We had it on the inside of the front door of our apartment. Uncle Roy and Grampa had dropped by, unannounced, as usual (the way we liked it), to take us all to lunch. While we were standing around in the living room, Uncle Roy pointed out Raquel to Grampa.

"Hey, Dad, see this?" Uncle Roy asked with the trademark Wilson smile. He awaited Grampa's reply. We all waited.

Grampa took a good, long look before asking, "Who is she?!"

"That's George's girlfriend." My roommate George was standing right there. He laughed, along with everyone else in the room. Except Grampa.

"Do you love her?" Grampa asked George in what seemed to be a very direct, almost scolding tone of voice.

"Well...sure I do, Mr. Wilson!" George said.

"Well then," continued my usually gentle Grampa, "why don't you buy her some clothes?!"

We all erupted in gales of painful laughter. Even Grampa enjoyed his own joke and joined the chorus of laughter. In a room full of tricksters, goofballs, and known sillies, my eighty-four-year-old Baptist grandfather had topped us all.

We were undone and outdone. I should not have been surprised, since he had fathered three dangerously comical sons and an authentically zany daughter, my Aunt Marcie. That the overwhelmingly sexual nature of the Raquel Welch photo had neither phased my Grampa nor missed his notice was a great delight. Before long, everyone in the Minneapolis College of Art and Design knew the story. It was thrice retold to me by people who were unaware that the story was about my Grampa. Lots of school chums and faculty knew I was a churchgoer, and this story did not quite fit their little collection of preconceptions about Christian believers.

Grampa Wilson's youngest son, my father, helped me learn the truth about my sexual self. He was a professional educator, athlete, gentleman, and relentless kidder. He was deeply spiritual, but never uptight or legalistic. He was not shocked or stopped by the world he lived in because he had been in the Navy, as had Uncle Roy.

I first heard about the basic mechanical details of sex from peers, but it was shortly explained, sorted out, and made clear by my mother and my father. They infused the basic mechanical details with a heaping helping of self-worth, dignity, and constant respect for the other person.

Even though my parents eventually helped me get the story straight, I still had to go up against the church, where many of its well-intentioned, though too tightly wound, members saw it as their place to warn us about the devil in blue suede shoes.

That night at the junior high candlelit make-out party, we moved beyond group events to the one-on-one, the free-style event. I wasn't looking to put my hands inside anyone's clothing. I just wanted to kiss my girlfriend, nice and slow, to remember every moment of it. No more quickly taken roller rink kisses or pecks-on-the-cheek-behind-the-hay-bales-at-camp kisses. It was grand.

Then, without warning, during one fairly long kiss and embrace, my girlfriend opened her mouth. It was automatic for me to open mine—I didn't think about it. Truth be told, it opened by itself. I had never opened my mouth while kissing before. And then it happened. Our tongues touched! O-O-O-Wow! I thought I had died and gone to...well, I didn't know where I was. We looked at each other—grinning, shocked, exhilarated, excited. We were scared to move on, and too eager not to. We had to do it again. We did. And did, and did, and...What was this? It was more than plain kissing, but it wasn't "heavy (sinful) petting" as described by the uptight righteous ones who would do away with fun as a safety measure. These holy humbuggers had never mentioned tongues-in-mouths during their hands-in-clothes speeches. Did this glorious practice live in a world between kissing and heavy petting, or was it beyond heavy petting on the way to "sleeping together"?

I decided to consult with experts—a couple of buddies who were the make-out kings of our school. Actually they were the two best-looking and most popular guys in the seventh grade, so they were imbued with expert status.

"How'd you guys make out the other night?" I asked in a voice so cool I might have been asking the contents of their lunch sandwiches.

"Great!" Les was certain.

"Fine." Gary was satisfied.

"What about you?" Les wanted to know.

"Let's just say..." Searching for just the right words without bragging, "it was a mouth-opening experience."

They got it, and shared that their evenings had been equally "mouth opening."

"And all this time I thought God had made tongues just for pronouncing consonants and the sounds th, ch, and sh." Leave it to me to find comedy in such an important, life changing experience.

"Nope," Gary quickly suggested, "God knew what he was doing."

"Think so?" Still worried about exactly where this appeared on the sin scale.

"Yup!" Les was at peace with the world on this.

That was good enough for me. Les and Gary were good friends, with decent reputations in the area of boy-girl relationships, they both knew and loved God and, more importantly, came from "nice" families.

To be absolutely certain I wasn't French kissing my way into the bottomless pit of eternal flames and homework, I decided to ask my mom. But, with no small amount of fear and trepidation.

"Mom, do you know," I began with a firmly clinched jaw, "what, ah, 'French kissing' is?"

"Yeah. Isn't it great!"

"Mother!" She had turned my sincere inquiry into a cheering session for my recently budding sex life. She went on to assure me that French kissing was not a sin. "Not even close." Although I believed her, I must say that her sincerity laced with playfulness left a trace of doubt in my mind. After all the Sunday sourpusses I'd grown up listening to who would outlaw all pleasure and were so relentless, so incessant in their forbidding of fun, I still worried that there was an outside chance that the naysayers may be right. Even so, they never mentioned French kissing. Besides, no matter what they might have to say, I had finally consulted a higher authority, my mom.

Onward Christian solders. Onward and upward.

11

Churchianity
Taking God to lunch

Life's a pudding full of plums.

—W. S. Gilbert

For many years of my life, Sunday was more about going to lunch than about going to church. Though I grew up in the moderately conservative "Evangelical" wing of Christianity, we were not so much concerned with sacrament and ceremony as we were with repentance and attendance. Nonetheless, we imbued going to lunch on Sunday with a devotion and ceremony accorded few other activities in life. We maintained a very short list of approved establishments where lunch was taken by the faithful, at least those within our circle of faith. Sunday lunch (in Minnesota my cousins go to "supper") is brought to you today by: Goodies Coffee Shop, Steak Corral, Northwoods Inn, Gus's Bar-B-Q, and Beadles cafeteria. All but the Steak Corral are still thriving in Southern California. The Steak Corral building is still standing, though now it's a Chinese restaurant — with virtually no change in decor.

As often as not, my family was joined for lunch by one or more other families. If it was a fancy "take-the-guest-preacher-to-lunch" Sunday we might go to the upscale Mexican restaurant El Poché. (Growing up on the right side of the body of Christ, the guest preacher was always a "him." Always. Except during Missionary Challenge Week when various wives might "share" a story from the "foreign fields," but they would most assuredly not preach.) Going to lunch with a Wilbur Smith, Torrey Johnson, J. Vernon Magee, or Louis Talbot required careful planning. They were and are legends.

Goodies Coffee Shop — too casual. The same held true for Beadles and Steak Corral — both cafeteria style. I grew up believing that famous preachers couldn't carry cafeteria trays or grab their own chocolate pudding. Cafeteria food was edible, so it had to be the carrying and lifting events that didn't work for them. Northwoods Inn, on the other hand, was the theme park of restaurants, but without the rides. (When they built one of the first Colonel Sanders' Kentucky Fried Chickens across the street from our church, the Colonel was added to the approved Sunday lunch options.)

Lunch with famous preachers or not-so-famous missionaries was, for my brother and me, about eating and listening. Eventually our quiet behavior called attention to itself and the famous guest would ask us about ourselves. Eventually, too — and far earlier than other parents would have allowed — my brother and I were permitted to join in the conversation whenever we had something to say. This especially included questioning the preacher on a point he'd made in the morning sermon. Most were actually amused with our curiosity and tenacity. My brother was curious; I did tenacious.

I once asked Dr. Louis Talbot — for whom Talbot Theological Seminary (at BIOLA University) was named — how he knew the Bible was all true if that was the only place where a lot of those stories were told. He told me that we believe it by faith. "No one can see God, but we believe in God," I remember him saying. "And so we believe God's Word, the Bible." But did he really believe that all that stuff happened just the way the Bible said it did? "Well, I believe God, and the Bible is God's Word."

There was, in that statement, more a ring of hope than of absolute certainty. I remember thinking that even if he didn't quite know if all of it was true or not, he wanted to believe it. I have always admired that kind of honesty from the clergy. That is, when I can find it.

Picking a place for lunch was integral to Sunday morning. As we always selected from the short list of approved eateries, I came to believe that families who went elsewhere might be of a slightly different faith than my family. At school, I had many friends who attended different churches. They all seemed to have their own set of Sunday lunch places. I imagined that each denomination had a list of sanctioned restaurants that went with their church's theological bent—their own Doctrine of Lunch. What puzzled me was families at our church who did not eat at the same places that we and our circle of friends did. I never did quiz any of the visiting doctrinal dignitaries to opine on the Doctrine of Lunch.

With our lifestyle so thoroughly and constantly hammered on by the church, you cannot help but come to believe that every activity of life is either God's way—the church way—or the "world's" way. We are taught that "as a person thinketh in their heart, so is he." To have hatred in our heart is to do murder, Christ taught. To lust is to commit adultery. Of course the only conclusion young churchgoers jump to is that if we're sinning just by thinking about it, and will get into trouble with God for it, anyway—just as much as if we actually did it—than why not *do it?* Not murder, but, y'know...*it.* Had I been raised Roman Catholic,

I imagined that going to the "wrong" Sunday lunch place might have been a venial, or lesser, sin. I suspect there are not a lot of folks in Purgatory doin' time for inappropriate Sunday luncheonette choices. I wonder what they serve for lunch in Purgatory? Actually I don't believe Purgatory exists. It's redundant. If Heaven is eternity in the presence of God, and Hell is eternal separation from God then what is Purgatory? If God is not there, it's a Hell of a place. What's the difference?

Just as Sunday lunch had its doctrinally correct and denominationally approved outposts, so, too, did after-the-evening-service dinner. Here, the list was shorter: In rhubarb season, Goodies got the night nod (for their prodigious pies), Baskin-Robbins for ice cream, El Taco for a late dinner, Me 'n' Ed's for pizza, and the-ever-popular Colonel for chicken. The Colonel was the only place that made both lunch and late-night lists — a Christian restaurant if there ever was one.

If that much import was attached to the mere selection of Sunday dining, you might only imagine the catalogue of demi-doctrines that were hatched in the mind of a young boy attending private school, church, Sunday school, and evening services every Sunday of his life.

Will There Be S'mores in Heaven?

Ergo all of life was plotted, experienced, and assessed through church-colored glasses. They filtered out options too closely aligned with the "world" and factored in choices that were safely church-related. It was as simple as planning a week of summer vacation at the beach or Yosemite National Park's White Wolf Camp to be enjoyed with other church families. Or a summer vacation week at family camp.

"That's not vacation!" I complained once, or thrice. "Family camp is Sunday school and church five days a week at five thousand feet above sea level." Church was already stifling enough, we didn't need to reduce the oxygen content as well. I liked every member of every family we ever camped, retreated, or beached with, but our lives became wall-to-wall Churchianity. Whether we were hiking the peaks of the Sierras or hanging on the sands of the Pacific, we were surrounded by church deacons, elders, trustees, pastors, and — with my family — the inescapable presence of the principal of the church school, my dad.

On many occasions, we invited many and all along the beach and through a campsite to join our evening do-it-ourselves campfire service. We'd have singing, skits, a Bible lesson, and s'mores! I believe my dad once quoted Jesus as saying, "I have come that you might have life, and that you might have it s'more abundantly." Works for me.

"Hey, Jesus, we're all out of marshmallows. Got any ideas?"

Our God squad getaways were not limited solely to summer vacations. Disneyland trips, Dodger games, even family movie nights involved churchgoers going together. We once went with about fifty people from our church to the famous Egyptian Theater in Hollywood to see the epic *Ben-Hur*, starring Charlton Heston, with a cameo appearance by Jesus. It was Sunday night church with popcorn.

12

101 Damnations

I met God at the movies

The meek shall inherit the earth.

—Jesus

The stupid share a studio apartment in the afterlife.

—McNair

There it was, loud and clear, in black and white, in the Sunday morning church bulletin: "Tonight at 6:00 p.m., Evening Service: Singing and Bible study, Pastor Franck preaching: '101 Damnations.'"

"Isn't that a bad word?" my brother and I asked. This was at a time when we were not permitted to say "shut up" around our house. As it turned out, a lot of families in our church were trying to answer the "damnation" question that Sunday afternoon on their way home from church. As a result, there was a larger than usual turnout that evening. Everyone wanted to know Pastor Franck's damn answer. Disney had just released it's animated classic, *101 Dalmatians.* Even though Pastor Franck was not an overly clever man, he hit pay dirt with this one. We all recognized the allusion, but few, if any, deduced his motives.

My father knew where his co-staff member was coming from. He'd been in the far corner of fundamentalist isolationism where morals are circumscribed so precisely you'd do best to stay at home. In his capacity as business manager of our church, my father was not only a fellow staff member with Pastor Franck, he was his surrogate landlord. The Francks lived in a small house, owned by our church and just across the street from the church offices. At least once a month, my father would walk across the street to visit the Francks and pick up their rent check. One Sunday evening, before the six o'clock service, my father popped across the street only to find the entire Franck family gathered around a warm television set — popcorn and other munchies in hand — preparing to watch the Sunday Night Movie on TV. "Movie Night at the Francks!" my dad announced lightheartedly. As Pastor Franck handed my father their rent check, my father asked him to step outside for a minute so he could chat with him outside the hearing of his family.

"So, it's family movie night, huh?"

"Yeah-heh-heh," Pastor Franck said. It was Sunday and they would be skipping church that evening to stay at home and watch the movie. My father had no problem with the Francks — or any family — staying home on a Sunday evening. My father was an educator by trade but supported families being together even if it meant keeping your kids out of school so the family could be together for almost any reason. He would say that being together was the top priority.

"Just a few weeks ago," my father began, once they were together on the front porch, "you stood before a full church and railed against moviegoing from the pulpit. Now here you are at home with your family to watch a big Hollywood movie. It seems fine to you to watch a movie on television in your home that just a while ago was in theatres. Is it the theatre building that is evil in your mind, the other people in the theatre, the popcorn?

Pastor Franck's "101 Damnations" was a rant on modern culture with his eyes fixed on movies as the primary evil in the land. This was not new information. Large numbers of church folk had been averse to moviegoing for decades. This was the early 1960s and many church families were by now regularly attending all sorts of movies.

My family were avid and regular movie-buffs. My brother and I saw every James Bond flick, western, musical, and everything Disney. My mother grew up in a non-legalistic church home and did not carry the "movies are evil" gene. She was aware of that breed of narrow-mindedness, but Pastor Franck's was the first time such religious non-think was unavoidably in her face. His sermon that Sunday night was very disturbing to my mother for he preached with loud and fiery conviction (condemnation). After years of movie and theatre going, she was suddenly filled with guilt. False guilt to be sure, but it had as strong a grip. Paralyzing. Life was quite taut at our house in the days following Pastor Franck's words of damnation. Days stretched into weeks. It lasted a couple of months, during which my brother and I did not see one movie in a theatre. My brother and I began to imagine that we might never see another movie in a theatre until our eighteenth birthday. We talked about sneaking away to a movie, but we were too young to drive and the closest movie house was a very long walk from our home. We decided to wait till our mom got over her affliction of guilt — or until we were old enough to drive.

Our father, meanwhile, was not similarly attacked by this virus of false guilt. He had been raised in a home afflicted with the malady of guilt associated with most all human pleasures. There is an insidious movement among church folk of all persuasions to ignore God's call to abate human suffering and, instead, to be about creating human suffering in the form of guilt—big, small, and false.

I asked our family doctor about this years ago when I was interested in becoming a doctor and curious about everything medical. Those interests passed, but in the meantime I asked Doc Hamilton about hypochondriacs. "How do you cure people who only imagine that they're sick? What medicine do you give them?"

He told me that the patients whose maladies are only in their mind are often the most difficult patients to care for. Placebos, long-term care, often even expensive procedures are administered to assure them that they are being attended to. Someone who is suffering from a known ailment can be attended to with the standard regimen for relief. But the imaginary invalid can be nearly impossible to treat.

My mother's guilt about going to movies, any movie, was not based in reality. It was conjured up in the moment of her ardent faith being kidnapped by the narrow non-think of another. She had been sidetracked on the road to Glory. My mother's lifelong faith in a grand and grace-filled God had been put in a stranglehold by the overwhelming frustration a minister wrestled with, and perhaps even a bit from being frightened by the world. For a while it occurred to us that the joy of our entire family was being choked off by Pastor Franck's rule-bound and baseless theology.

We didn't go to movies for a long time.

At that time, the State Theater on Colorado Blvd., in our town of Pasadena, California, specialized in exhibiting cinema classics. One Tuesday evening, during my mom's bout with conscience, we were all having dinner, and my dad asked my brother and me if we had gone to see the *Huck Finn* yet. We had not. We had been afraid to say anything about going to the movies in front of our mom while she was still having this collision of conscience and faith.

"*Huck Finn,* with Mickey Rooney. It's a classic, honey." My dad nudged gently.

"I know, but I'm still not comfortable—"

"Isn't this the last night for *Huck Finn?*" my dad asked us.

"Yeah," we told him. "They change the movies every Wednesday."

"This is the last night to see it on the big screen." He looked at my mom. Not like an order, it was more of a plea. My dad never ordered or bossed anyone.

"But this is a school night!" my mom said. We never, ever went to movies on a school night, so of course we weren't going to change that now, especially with all the soul-searching theological grappling my mom was doing.

Throughout this whole crisis of conscience for my mother, at no point had my dad told her what to do or how to think about what Pastor Franck had said. Eventually—after it was all behind us — my dad revealed that he stood in clear and unambiguous opposition to Pastor Franck's philosophy on moviegoing and related non-issues of the faith. My dad disagreed even more with the decision to deliver so provocative a sermon in a family service.

Even though Pastor Franck was not our "senior pastor," the title "pastor" anywhere in church circles carries a level of influence and, therefore, authority that has been abused and misused. In far too many cases, professional ministry folk have misappropriated their influence over the faithful to push an agenda that was not God's or — in the worst-case scenarios — to promote themselves, enlarge personal fortunes, and satisfy carnal desires. We need look no farther than our television sets to see crises of ego among servants of God. I fear the final chapter in that book is a long way from completion.

I will never forget what my dad said on that critical last night of *Huck Finn*'s visit to Pasadena. In response to my mom's mournful, "It's a school night," he looked right at my mom and said, *"Huck Finn."*

"But—"

"God can't possibly be against *Huck Finn*."

"I'm sure God is in favor of *Huck Finn,*" my mom conceded.

Moments later, we were in the station wagon with my mom headed uptown to the movies—on a school night!

Even though she believed in us going to see *Huck Finn* on this particular night, she remain troubled about movies in general — as a direct result of Pastor Franck's Damnations. Her prayers for God's guidance continued even as we headed to the movies.

Walking up to the stand-alone box office, beneath the State Theater's dancing neon marquee, there was a very short line to purchase tickets. We weren't in a line a moment when my mom suddenly realized she knew the patron directly in front of us in line. It was neither a neighbor nor a relative.

"Dr. Talbot?" My mom tapped the older gentlemen on the shoulder.

"Yes?" Immediately, as he turned to speak to her, his face lit up with the surprise of bumping into an old friend. "Mrs. Wilson! And the boys."

"Hello, Dr. Talbot." My mother was shocked to see at a movie theatre the man for whom one of Christendom's most respected theological training schools — Talbot Seminary — was named. "I must say I am surprised to find you here...at the movies."

"It's *Huck Finn,* one of the best," he exclaimed. "I'm here with my daughter and grandson."

"But do you go to movies much?" My mom would squeeze as much from this moment as possible.

"Why everybody needs to see a good motion picture show now and then. Especially in a theatre, with a big screen, and some good popcorn," he said.

Dr. Talbot had preached in the pulpit of our church. He had been to dinner at our house, but on this one particularly magical evening, Dr. Louis Talbot needed to say no more. Little did he know that as far as my mom was concerned, on that night, he spoke for God. He often spoke for God as a nationally known preacher with a fiery style and quick wit. His gentle endorsement of moviegoing was as clear an answer to prayer as my mother ever got from her Lord. She said that whenever she retold this story over the subsequent years.

Talbot Seminary was a sister institution with, and shared the campus of, BIOLA College (now University.) Ironically, back then—the 1960s—students and *faculty* of BIOLA were not allowed to go to movies during their time at BIOLA. Dr. Talbot's influence was not absolute—even when he was right.

This incident changed our family, absolutely.

13

Drawing in Church
And other traditions of the faith

Paint as you like and die happy.
—Henry Miller

It's all my parent's fault. They started me at a very early age. Actually, I have the life I chose and continue to create, born of my choices. My parents may have indeed gotten me started, but I chose to press on. And so I did.

I confess. I doodle in church. Heck, I doodle, sketch, and draw everywhere. All the drawings in this book are mine. Every one lifted from one of more than 140 sketchbooks. Anyone who knows me or has been around me knows that I am never without my sketchbook. I draw everywhere — and on everything—napkins, paper towels, business cards, place mats, small children. . . .

When I was very young, my brother and I started going to "big church" with our parents rather than to "junior church" with our peers. Sitting through a one-hour-fifteen-minute church service when you are only five years old is less riveting than virtually every other activity in the life of a five year old — except the decidedly un-riveting "junior church." To make the time pass less irksomely, my mom introduced the delightful diversion of doodling on the blank backside of offering envelopes. When he didn't have platform duties, my father took up the doodling gaunt-let, enthusiastically drawing along. My father was not the artist that my mother was. But, in church, my dad was Rembrandt with a golf pencil. Mostly he copied my mom's doodles.

Our early drawings were of freight trains—circus trains with boxcars carrying animals. There was always a chug of smoke spewing from the engine, followed by a heaping coal car and the heads of exotic animals poking through every opening—giraffe, elephant, rhinoceroses, horses. Fi-nally, a caboose. Often, our trains were of such a length that they began on one offering envelope and continued onto others—like a train.

Eventually I stopped doodling trains and started paying attention to the service. I did not discontinue drawing. In-stead, I drew what was going on around me. There was no end to interesting subjects to draw both in church and especially in the sermon.

By contrast, I did relatively little doodling in school. Mostly it was daydreaming that occupied my academic free time. In church, though, I doodled. In the racks of of-fering envelopes and visitor registration cards were also sheets of note paper in the form of the blank backs of recycled flyers that had once stuffed the Sunday morn-ing bulletins. This was well before anyone knew the word "recycle" and certainly long before it was hip. It was just "scratch paper."

All of this doodling and drawing went on in full view of my parents. To say that I had their permission is to seriously understate their role. Their participation was com-plete. Many a Sunday there was an old bulletin insert or flyer thrust upon me by my mom or dad, even before we sat

Todd (brother), Craig (moi), Donna (mother), Joe (pastor), Wils (my dad's nickname, from Wilson). My dad sat behind Pastor Joe and reeled his microphone cord in and out as he paced the platform. This drawing, dated "Craig 1960"—Dad's writing—I drew when I was seven years old.

down in our every-Sunday, left side, center pew, our "regular" pew. They knew I could redesign, rewrite, and recycle a funner, funnier version of the upcoming 14th annual Torrey Memorial Bible Conference.

Regular pew is a way of church members keeping track of one another: who's here and who's not ("I wonder where the Fitzgeralds are today?) In the summer, we track vacations. ("Did Bernice go back East to her sisters' again? Wasn't she just there in March?") *Regular pew* was quite an effective means of checking up on each other.

Finally, and it was fairly early on as a kid, I did pay attention to what was being said, sung, and sermonized. Then my doodles turned from circus to substance. Fellini-esque characters filled the pews and peopled the platform. Those early images formed the foundation for the recurring citizenry in my doodling to this day.

The easiest task is always creating a cartoon version of a story plucked from the minister's sermon. Easy, but often redundant because a story is an illustration, a word picture. The better challenge is to pick up on a phrase, an aside, a throwaway comment and aim my felt-tipped spotlight on that — making it a larger, more important point. Many a minister has felt the felt-tipped point of my satire.

Giving significance to the insignificant is a regular practice of cartoonists and satirists. With me, it's a passion.

The highlighting of smaller moments in a larger, well-crafted sermon gets the biggest response from preachers, pastors, and guest speakers with whom I almost always share my drawings. Usually they smile, laugh, even frown. My favorite response is surprise. This comes when I have been listening close enough to detect a personal rant subplot that has worked itself into the sermon as an aside. I transform it into the primary theme of my drawing.

Cartoons are anger made helpful. A syndicated political cartoonist I enjoy describes his job as "getting angry six times a week." To be sure, I am not always angry when I create a cartoon. Would that more of the world's problems could be so easily relieved by some few simple strokes of a felt pen across the blank page of a cartoonist's sketchbook.

Next weekend, as you're thumbing through the Sunday funnies, notice how virtually every comic strip is a tiny dose of our own reality recycled for our enjoyment. They are us, turned sideways, like a bent and crooked full-length mirror in front of a carnival fun house. A catharsis occurs for many women I know when they get their weekly fix of "Cathy" going through precisely the same stuff they are wrestling with everyday. Who among us doesn't know some of the same idiots and shysters that plague old *B.C.?* Who hasn't had a boss like the Wizard of Id or a co-worker like *Shoe;* or relationships like the long-suffering Herman? We have all gone through the I'm-a-grown-up-adult-intellectual phase

[overheard whilst crossing the parted-waters of the Red Sea.]

when we announced to our friends that we now find *Peanuts* simplistic or just don't find it funny anymore. But we have all found ourselves among Charles Schulz's gang. Whether its the negativism and self-aggrandizement of Lucy van Pelt, or Charlie, who was co-dependent before it was fashionable, or the brooding, introverted, self-pitying, troubled soul of Schroeder, all the time longing for the devil-may-care abandon, the joie de vivre of the perennially swashbuckling Snoopy. We are them, they are us.

When we get right down to it, Gary Larson might as well be drawing his cartoons about the Far Side of the church as about the cave people, forest animals, and residents of the reptile kingdom. Aren't all his kooky scientists, gathered around the chalkboard trying to figure out the meaning of life, the same bunch of early theologians that a twelve-year-old Jesus confounded with his simplicity? Don't all those chalk-wielding wizards still congregate and conjugate in buildings marked "seminary"?

It is to that grand tradition that I humbly submit an all too brief sampling of my view from the pew drawings of church characters and caretakers. Along the way, some of my church drawings were reconfigured and published in the ever-popular pages of *The Door* Magazine (*www.thedoormagazinecom*) — formerly *The Wittenburg Door* (1970–1989) and other periodicals of courage and silliness. A whole bunch of them got together and became my first book, *YHWH Is Not a Radio Station In Minneapolis* (HarperSanFrancisco, 1983.) More were assembled with the publishing of my book *Everyone Wants to Go to Heaven, But…: Wit, Faith, and a Light Lunch* (PageMill Press, 2000).

The doodling continues.

On these pages are a few of my favorites, taken from over 140 sketchbooks and two thousand Sunday mornings, Sunday evenings, conferences, retreats, Bible studies, and late night coffee shop theological roundtable talk-a-thons — non-smoking, please, we're church folk.

All drawings throughout this book are culled from those sacred sketches.

Most of the doodles stand alone — sans explanation. A few carry a line or two, added for these pages, to place them in context — just in case you missed that Sunday. Some I include for personal reasons, in which case I may be the only one laughing. Not to worry. As the old saying goes, some jokes you do just for yourself. Some, I hope, will just make you go, "Hmmmmm." I like that, too.

14

Climb Every Mountain

Actus non facit reum, nisi mens sit rea*

> It isn't that they can't see the solution.
> It is that they can't see the problem.
>
> —G. K. Chesterton

Mountain Christian Academy was not prepared to have me as a student. It was a well-established institution, a thriving enterprise.

Many of the students had been at Mountain Christian all their academic lives. Some of the teachers had once been students there. (This cycle is not uncommon going from Christian school to Christian college, and back to the Christian school as faculty — they're "mutant Christians" and they have been known to intermarry.) Several families had been involved in the formation of the school, and the fathers were school board members for *life.*

Although I had attended private, church-related schools since kindergarten, and my mom and dad had been teacher and principal in a large private school, I had never run up against anything like Mountain Christian. I had certainly heard about such places. One of the great indoor sports that my family played was "What's the latest stupid rule you've heard about Bob Jones University."

---

*There is no guilty act without a guilty mind.

99

Bob Jones University is a real place in Greenville, S.C. It is a large, conservative "Christian" university that has turned fundamentalism into a science. They have rules to govern every activity in life, from breathing, to walking, and thinking. Dating is a "no bodily contact" event, done in the BJU "dating lounge," and is never inter-racial. For the longest time African-Americans were not admitted as students. The campus is a fenced-in, guarded encampment. In an interview with Larry King, university president Bob Jones Jr. was asked by a teenage caller (regarding inter-racial dating), "My mother is white and my father is black. If I were to attend your school, which race would I be allowed to date?"

Larry King added, with no hidden enthusiasm, "Great question!"

"Well...." Dr. Jones was noticeably stumped. "You, ah, you...would be welcome to be a student at Bob Jones University, and would be allowed to date...ah...whichever race that you most closely resembled."

Wow! He could not have been clearer about what he really believes.

When I told my parents about actually hearing this exchange with my own ears, we laughed, roared, and screamed. My dad shook his head saying, "Those guys just won't learn."

Meanwhile, back in my youth....My brother and I would soon realize that Mountain Christian Academy (MCA) bore more than a passing resemblance to Bob Jones. Both of MCA's vice principals had attended Bob Jones — one had even taught there—and had brought too much of Bob Jones with them. The founding principal (still there when we arrived) had attended the Bible Institute of Los Angeles, a.k.a. BIOLA. Unlike Bob Jones, though, BIOLA University had grown up, some, modifying many of its severest notions. BI-OLA had, apparently, read farther into the New Testament. Keep reading, everybody!

My mother and father, quite relaxed about lifestyle, never flinched when my brother or I dated Asian, black, Hispanic, or Jewish girls. My first experience with tobacco was aided by my dad and uncle, and my parents told me the plain truth about sex long before my hormones were interested. My parents did flinch, however, when they first looked into Mountain Christian. They were called in for a "parents' interview" prior to being allowed to enroll us, apparently to see if "we" were the kind of family they wanted.

My father told them, "The boys and their mother will be at the interview together." Though the administration protested, Todd and I accompanied our mom for our first peek at Mountain Christian Academy. One lasting, strong first impression was that whenever my brother or I asked a question (we asked a lot of questions), the answer was always directed at our mother as though we weren't even there.

"Do you have any questions, Mrs. Wilson?"

"The boys will be here every day," she said, "It's up to them to ask and decide if they want to go here."

Behind the scenes, my mother was given a copy of the student handbook to look over with my dad, but was instructed not to show it to us as "the boys, will get one on the opening day of classes." That was enough for my mom to decide that she didn't want us to attend there. She and my dad agreed to say nothing about these feelings and to wait for Todd and me to form our own opinions.

That was standard operating procedure in our family on just about everything. As far back as the summer before my fourth grade year, when I was just nine years old, my folks asked my brother and me if we'd like to switch to public school. We had been attending the private church school where my dad was the principal. We made a visit to the local public school, talked to the teachers, examined their text books, recess schedule, lunch room, etc. I even made a couple of round trips on my bike and one on foot to check out the four-block journey. I also interviewed kids in the neighborhood, listing pros and cons on a long legal pad my dad gave me, with clipboard. I chose to return to San Gabriel Christian that year. The conversation regarding public or private school went on every year, throughout the year, until I finished high school, even after I finally chose to switch to public school.

I always believed I would stay in private school through high school. That was before Mountain Christian Academy. The next two years were to be the most dramatic of my entire educational career. It is a time that, to this day, is difficult—painful even—to recall.

My brother was a freshman beginning his high school career. I was a sophomore and had already spent one year at Pacific Christian, an outstanding small church-related high school in Los Angeles. That summer, our family had moved to the Bay Area. The move itself was also a choice the whole family had voted on. Dallas was the second-place winner, receiving, as I recall, zero votes.

Our odyssey began the first day of the fall semester. The combined junior and senior high student bodies assembled in the chapel for faculty introductions and what started out like a normal chapel service—hymns, prayer, and flag salutes, Christian and American.

Then they passed out the student handbook. The first few pages covered procedures for tardiness, absenteeism, medical leave, class attendance, eligibility for extra curricular activities, and so on. All fairly standard stuff. We turned the page and the earth moved.

There, in what seemed like an endless list, were the rules for conduct and behavior. There were no less than twenty-six (count 'em: twenty-six) rules. God gave ten rules to cover all of human behavior. But the razor sharp, concrete-clad minds that governed Mountain Christian Academy figured out two and a half times as many absolutes for the deportment of the teenagers in their care. As is the case in many fundamentalist schools — high schools and colleges — the rules are to be adhered to on and off campus, weekends and holidays as well. Many a student has been expelled from a church-related school for "breaking the rules" during summer break, far away from campus.

As remarkable as the rules themselves were, the men's dean spent over an hour reading the student handbook at us. It was printed clearly, in English, but as a key to their total lack of trust in us, they read it to us word for word. Appropriate annotation and emphases were interjected all along the way, just so "there be no mistaking our intentions." That phrase, coupled with the harsh nasal twang of a southern preacher, made the hearing of these mostly preposterous rules all the more degrading. I told my folks later that I was embarrassed for him.

I remember thinking at the time that not one of these twenty-six rules mentioned or even alluded to us being good Christians, followers of Christ. There was not even a paraphrase of the biblical golden rule "do unto others as you would have them do unto you." That would not have sufficiently covered the many concerns of their suspicious minds. Not even a whisper that behavior guided by the Creator God was the order of the day. None of the other four church-related schools I had attended came close to so prescriptive a laying out of human behavior.

Among their twenty-six concerns, MCA mandated that there be "no spitting on walls, lockers, or other students." Pretty particular. I learned to appreciate the specificity of "walls, lockers, other students," as I was to come up against this rule that first year. My mother remarked at dinner that evening, "So, you *can* spit on teachers."

Two of the rules were the most jarring: numbers four and twenty-six. I could not have prepared myself for rule number four:

> We discourage the relationship of "going steady." This includes the exchanging of tokens, hand-holding, and all other such bodily contact.

As this rule was read aloud to us that opening day in September by "Coach" Davidson (vice-principal, dean of men, athletic coach, teacher and pastor of a small local "Bible Church"), I reacted audibly, "You're kidding me?!" It was a reflex without forethought. I could not believe what I was hearing. At least I didn't want to believe it.

My generation had been exchanging St. Francis medals (more a part of the surfing culture than anything Roman Catholic) for years. "Hand-holding" started for me and my peers in sixth grade, maybe earlier, and I was not the class pioneer on the hand-holding front.

There I was, near the back of the chapel, sitting among the sophomores (Class of '70), surrounded by cute girls and a pleasant crop of guys and I thought, and said, for all to hear, "You're kiddin' me?!"

Everything stopped. Everyone looked. One of the cuter girls, later to become my girlfriend, caught my eye and smiled. Several laughed, embarrassed. Mr./Rev./Coach

Davidson looked up from his reading of "holy scripture" like some ancient headmaster burst from the pages of Dickens and out across a sea of tight-butted boys in the drafty hall of an old English boarding school, "Ah...what...ah, is there ah...question?"

Well, of course there was, but by now I was beginning to catch on to the rather disquieting fact that I was at Bob Jones Academy West. Any minute now, the guards would come and fit us for ankle chains and medieval chastity belts. I did not pursue the debate. Not the first day. Nonetheless, the gauntlet had been thrown down. It would not be ignored.

Rather than helping us with our raging adolescent hormones, they chose to ignore them. More insidiously, even, they were mandating we deny emotion, biology, and make sexuality wrong on all counts. Even the most innocent practice, hand-holding, was banished to the lake of fire with all desires of the flesh. Just forget that you are becoming men and women. You are not here to be a person; you are students, athletes, and choir members, so keep your hands to yourself and your knees together.

Along the way, and with some guidance from my parents, I had put the boy-girl thing into a healthier perspective. There was still more to learn, but I was not going to learn it as a student at Mountain Christian. In fact, I was to leave there in some ways less healthy than when I arrived. Their childish attitudes were to become mine, and they would be attitudes I would hate in myself even more than I loathed them in them.

There was a disconnect in their understanding of the heart. Oh, they would be quick to share the time-honored metaphor that Jesus lived in our hearts, but they didn't want us to tell Jesus about our feelings. Don't ask Jesus about love or hand-holding or sexual arousal. And while we're not asking, don't ask the administration why healthy, God-fearing teenagers can't hold hands in the idyllic environs of a Christian school.

Of course, eventually I did ask directly, indirectly, and by my rule-breaking actions.

First, though, a look at the biggest piece of resistance in the MCA handbook: Rule No. 26. After enduring more than two hours of being read "at" like so many cross-legged pre-schoolers sitting on a hooked rug, the last rule pulled that rug right out from under us.

Rule 26: "Anything else that faculty, staff or adminis-tration determines to be detrimental to life at Moun-tain Christian Academy."

That's right, *anything else*... that comes up along the way.

"Anything else?" We were prisoners in a fenceless camp being told not to leave camp, but never shown the camp boundaries. Our lives were to be scrutinized moment-by-moment, and in any one of those moments we might be busted. It would not be long before "anything else" and I would become old friends.

Following the reading of rule twenty-six, I honestly ex-pected the Rev. Mr. Coach Davidson to ask for questions. Remember, I was new here. I'd grown up in a family where questions and dialogue were the order of the day. The other private schools I had attended, all church-related, provided room for questions. Not here. Nonetheless, I had questions, lots of them. In the coming months I would find a hun-dred different ways to ask them. I received few satisfactory answers. Worse, I was made wrong for asking.

Before we even had a chance to process the opening day chapel and rule fest, it was off to our first first-period. The surprises that MCA had to offer were just beginning.

Enter Jean Pruitt, history teacher. Young, dark, full of the kind of energy that sophomore boys don't need from a woman teacher. A teacher who began the first class perched on the front of her desk, legs crossed with more leg and knee showing than the now-legendary student handbook permits. Her opening salvo thickened the plot. "The cause of all wars...is love."

Silence. Stunned, uncomfortable silence.

To say we were confused doesn't cover it. Mostly, we didn't understand her point. What we did understand was that Mrs. Pruitt was new here, too. She would not last. We would talk about the history of the world all year with Jean Pruitt and look at it through the loves, the passions, and the belief systems of a hundred cultures and peoples. She was unorthodox in an institution of narrowly drawn certainties of orthodoxy. In their mad attempts to shelter us from the questions and passions of the world, the administration had left a window open. Like a cold, brisk, breath of winter air, Jean Pruitt blew into our lives, hearts, and minds with questions. Questions we had never heard. The firm foundation that MCA had been built on was shaking beneath us. Some were shaken by their inaugural trip down the rocky road of Doubt. Their fears were later shared with their parents who phoned the school to complain and, more likely, to threaten. Quicker than you could say "constituency," Mrs. Jean Pruitt was told (fundamentalists never ask, they tell) to change her tune. But not before she had brought in a guest singer — literally.

Live from the math department, on his full-sized Martin twelve string, the professor of protest, the geologist of jive, the tenor of the isosceles triangle, Mr. Tom Fagan (real name). One day we came into Mrs. P's small, windowless classroom, and there was quirky old Mr. F—the first person I knew personally who sported a goatee. This was 1967, and we were at a conservative fundamentalist private Christian school. A goatee-free zone.

That day's lesson was the American protest song. He sang pro-labor songs, civil right songs, anti-(Viet Nam) war songs; you name it, Mr. Fagan sang it. On "Where Have All the Flowers Gone?" he beckoned us "sing along if you know it." Those who did, did. (Just Beth Endsley and me.) Everyone knew "We Shall Overcome." Barely a handful sang along. But when Mr. Fagan launched into Country Joe McDonald's "1–2–3 What Are We Fightin' For?" the protest turned on him.

> And it's 1–2–3 what are we fightin' for?
> Don't ask me I don't give a damn,
> Next stop is Viet Nam....

"Are you against the war, Mr. Fagan?" asked Ronnie Crandall, more confused than upset. Ronnie's question set off a barrage of questions that grew angrier and angrier.

Mr. Fagan tried to explain that the protest song had been a part of our American social-political landscape since the Revolutionary War. No one had questioned his singing "Battle Hymn of the Republic."

Mr. Fagan would be silenced, too. He would not again be asked to lead singing in chapel. He was a very good guitar player. He was enthusiastic about singing and playing the guitar. He was enthusiastic about math and God and life!

He didn't stop singing, though. At night, after school, he would sit on the porch of his home in the Santa Cruz mountains and sing. I heard him almost every night. Mr. Fagan, you see, lived with my family that first year. His mother had worked for my dad in Southern California. She was my sixth grade teacher. She was from Ireland, and you could hear the lilt in her voice. She, too, was a great teacher. She taught ancient history like she'd been there.

The story gets more complicated when you know that my father had written a glowing letter of recommendation for Mr. Fagan when he applied to teach at MCA — inasmuch as Tom Fagan had been a substitute math and geography teacher at my dad's school. One morning, while substituting in my seventh grade geography class, he brought in some rocks and fossils that suggested that the world was a lot older than most conservative Christians wanted it to be. That was fine with my dad. "Makes you think!" he most likely said at supper that night.

All this is to say that Mr. Fagan was a good teacher, a great teacher. Like his mother before him, he loved his subject and teaching. Singing American folk and protest songs was part of his teaching.

Over the next couple of years, I would meet several teachers who were filled with that same enthusiasm and a genuine lust for life, more life than the tightly wound school board and administration at MCA were prepared to accept. More life than their handbook of twenty-six certainties allowed. Finally, it was more life than they were able to endure.

They didn't like the idea of crayons, let alone coloring outside the lines. For them the final *Jeopardy* answer was always, "Because we said so."

In John's poetic retelling of the Gospel account, he records Jesus saying, "I have come that you might have life, and that you might have it *more* abundantly." MCA, like far too many other church-related academies of their bent, was mostly about less. Less thoughtful, less joyful, less abundant life—even non-abundance. They are life-less. That restrictive, mind-choking, spirit-abusing institutions like this continue to exist is almost more curious than is the insufferable narrowness of their views. Alas, religious fundamentalism is alive and thriving in American culture as well as their more-famous counterparts in Eastern cultures.

Fundamentalism — whether it is the extraordinary silliness of Bob Jones University or the terrorism of a fundamentalist jihad — is a lonely place. In the religious world, fundamentalists even cut themselves off from each other. They talk about such things as "church purity" and "rightly dividing the word of truth." But only *their* stridently redefined truth will suffice. They even make a sport of trying to "out-fundamental" one another:

"We don't ordain women."

"We don't let women teach."

"We don't let women speak."

"We think women have cooties!"

In the Apostle Paul's correspondence to believers in Rome, the New Testament's rich and restorative Book of Romans, he states unhesitatingly at the beginning of letter (chapter) fourteen:

Don't turn away other believers from worshiping with you, just because they don't believe exactly the way you do. (Romans 14:1, *The Message,* a contemporary setting of the Older and Newer Testaments by Eugene Peterson)

Somehow, though, fundamentalists find a way to slam their doors on the faces and fingers of any and all who do not agree with them. No discussion, get out! As far as the administration at MCA knew, their beliefs were based on a literal reading of the Bible. Eventually, this so-called literalism became a cause called "inerrancy."

Along with this strict, literal, rigid interpretation of the Bible, the inerrancy movement was accompanied by an attitude. They would answer questions by quoting scripture. Invoking the word of God, speaking for God, was a daily occurrence at Mountain. And when a Bible verse was used, as it almost always was, you knew that to ask another question was to question God.

Don't shoot the messenger if he is a messenger of God. Did Mr. Davidson and other administrators speak for God? They did — absolutely! On this subject more than any other—their authority—they once again invoked holy writ, "The present authority [themselves] is of God." To this day, that phrase rings in my ears like the deafening toll of an enormous cathedral bell announcing the coronation or, more likely, the beheading of a monarch. I really have only heard that verse a couple of times outside of my years at Mountain, but while there, I heard it virtually every week. It was actually used three times in one conversation. Ringing, ringing, ringing!

"The present authority is of God." That is to say, we are in charge. Do not question us. God put us here. Finally, I had to ask the fatal, never-before-asked follow-up question. So I asked, "Was Dietrich Bonhoeffer (a German Christian) wrong to plot the assassination of Adolf Hitler? Was Hitler the 'present authority of God'?"

"Are you saying we're Hitler?"

"Fine. Forget Hitler," I jumped back in, trying to save my ever-shortening neck. "Were the Puritans out of line to flee religious persecution for freedom in the New World? Should they have accepted the present authority over them, no matter how oppressive? And didn't Moses lead the children of Israel out of Egyptian bondage? Was the present authority, Pharaoh, of God?"

They didn't get it. I was neither a Puritan nor an Egyptian slave, and they were not oppressive, old world monarchs. But oppressive and old world is exactly what they were. They tossed scripture at us like papal edicts. I felt like Martin Luther being "gored" by a papal bull. In this and dozens of other instances where I stood before the Mountain Christian Sanhedrin, I was wrong, out of line, and "sowing discord among the brethren."

They could nose-dive into their Bible and emerge with a phrase for any occasion. According to them, I had given them more such occasions than they had ever needed to explain and defend themselves. During one of several visits my father made — mostly at the administration's invitation — he was told that never before had a student given them so much trouble with their rules and policies. They implied that no one had ever before questioned them on anything.

Not so, said my girlfriend, who had grown up in that school. Most who questioned were suppressed or squeezed out. She also told me that students complained about the rigid code of conduct and ever-expanding list of absolutes all the time, but never out loud. They also knew which of their classmates not to complain around: someone whose father was on the school-board-for-life (only fathers were on the board), an unofficial cast of Brahmans.

"That's why they interview parents," my father volunteered. He had realized from the beginning of our relationship with Mountain that they knew that not everyone belonged there. As life on the mountain got tougher for me, my folks were more forthcoming with their initial fears.

I should tell you that both my brother and I found MCA repressive, but my brother is the strong, silent type. I remember his squinting, high-cheeked grin as we left chapel the first day, and he looked at me and shook his head as if to say, "They're hopeless, they're silly." I wanted to say to him, "Let's go over the wall now, while there's still a chance."

Most curious of all developments was that behind my troubles was a fear on the part of the shepherds of this lock-step flock of young lambs that my brother and I were doing our father's bidding. Whenever we raised a fuss, they honestly believed that two boys, ages fourteen and fifteen, were operatives in a covert scheme to undermine and bring down the "Mountain."

My father, you see — C. Elwood Wilson — served as president of the California Association of Christian Schools in the 1960s and was on the board of directors for the National Association of Christian Schools. As gentle a man as he was, his creative acumen and wisdom as an educator were famous and ferocious. He gained a level of influence, authority, and flat-out clout that went with him no matter what his specific professional title was at any given moment. He was known and respected for his talent and innovation in educational circles across partisan and sectarian lines. He knew and was known by top educational leaders and state officials. He knew and was known by the officials at Mountain Christian — long before we even considered the move into that area.

So it was, with the combination of my father's considerable reputation and my larger-than-life personality, that the "present authorities" at Mountain Christian Academy had convinced themselves that, like the James Boys in the Old West, the Wilsons had ridden into town and the revolution had begun.

15

The Cartoon Heard 'Round the World
The day the bubble burst

> You see, but you do not observe.
>
> —*Adventures of Sherlock Holmes,*
> "Scandal in Bohemia"

A Baptist preacher, a Catholic priest, and a Jewish rabbi are floating in a raft in the middle of the ocean....

Laughter, in our family, was a form of communication, a means of navigating through life's rough and turbulent waters.

At its best, humor in my family was satire used to make a not-so-easily-swallowed point on a controversial issue. As often as not, we were satirizing the church soloist, visiting preacher, or latest "Christian movie." (How does a spool of celluloid become a Christian?)

How many televangelists does it take to change the tire on a Rolls Royce?

Mostly, the family comedy hour was held at our round, glass-top kitchen table. These comedy conversations were more like script sessions for the writing team of a TV sitcom.

It didn't take much to get the ball rolling. "Did you hear what (goofy televangelist) said on TV last Sunday?" We took turns satirizing a statement or event and carrying it to its logical, most absurd conclusion. Such is the basis for

114

the social-political-cultural satire of prophetic *MAD* magazine. Try re-reading *MAD* magazine from two or three years ago and you will discover that much of the silly extremes they went to have become the way things really are today.

A good bit of life is its own punch line. The satirist's task is to point out the absurdity, the extremism already inherent, though not completely apparent. It is then that comedy becomes terrifying. It was not necessary to change or satirize Oral Roberts's assertion that a nine-hundred-foot Jesus appeared to him in a vision telling him to build a huge hospital that Tulsa, Oklahoma, did not need. It was built and today it stands empty.

I believe in visions and revelations. I believe that God "speaks" to human beings today. In the New Testament, God speaks to Paul through an ass. My mom would say, "Thus establishing a practice that continues to this day." I also believe truth is truth, whether it's spray painted on a wall, sung by the rock band U2, or preached from a pulpit. At the same time, I have heard enough non-truth from pulpits to last an eternity. Maybe in Eternity, we will sit at round glass-top tables in the Heaven's breakfast nook and satirically recycle centuries of non-truth.

A lawyer dies and goes to Heaven.... (Now that's funny.)

Jesus used satire to get at the truth of a judgmental spirit when he suggested to the man that he might better see a speck in another man's eye, if he would first remove the two-by-four from his own eye. To miss Jesus' humor is to miss his point. But we don't want God to be funny. We think it is somehow ungodly to be funny.

If comedy is the extreme—and it often is—then it is more comedic than anything else for God to create an escape route for the children of Israel, being pursued by the armies of Pharaoh, by parting the deep and ferocious waters of the

Red Sea. Certainly as interpreted in Cecil B. DeMille's epic film *The Ten Commandments,* it is an awesome and terrifying moment. Step back for a moment and see the clever, absurd, silly truth of the act. The human comedy.

Early on, my humor became visual—doodling and drawing. I did it everywhere, and church was no exception (see chapter 13, "Drawing in Church"). Turning life into a cartoon has always been a regular and natural part of my personal expression.

Soon after my arrival at Mountain Christian Academy, I became editor-in-chief of the school newspaper. I knew I would create cartooned comments as a regular part of my work on the paper because I had drawn cartoons for student papers and yearbooks since fifth grade.

What I could never have anticipated was the monstrously negative environment MCA would be for me as a person and more particularly as an artist.

Chapels were held five days a week and our most frequent speaker was Vice-Principal/Coach/Reverend Davidson. He was a few verses to the right of Nebucadnezzar (of fiery furnace fame and flame.)

One Monday Mr. D announced he would be giving a week-long series on the value and virtue of Christian education over public education. In that first sermon he said, "public, or pagan, schools...." He repeated the word "pagan" just after saying public, several times until, finally, he said only pagan schools — omitting the word "public" altogether. The balance of the week, he spoke only of the evils and inferiority of *pagan* schools as contrasted with Christian schools. This was an important distinction when he stopped using the word "public" the very first day. I knew, too, that both my mother and father started their teaching careers in public, ah...pagan, schools, and that several other students at Mountain had parents who were currently "pagan schoolteachers."

Knowing my parents were in violent opposition to this philosophy, I gave nightly updates at our comedy round tables. They chose not to speak up, for now, but instead to let Mr. Davidson deliver his entire treatise. They would reserve judgment until after Friday's chapel. I was a sophomore and was not so patient.

After two or three days of his incessant pagan-bashing, classmates began using the term in casual conversation. "When I went to pagan school...." Some spoke in jest, but Mr. Davidson's harangue was taking root in the collective subconscious.

Growing up in the church, I learned to let truth-teller preachers and teachers carry on above reproach. So much so, that we'd never even think of questioning their words. When we didn't understand, it was assumed that it was we who had failed and lacked understanding or wisdom. It could not possibly be the speaker—and, in fact, it never was the speaker. Or so was the pervasive assumption we grew up to believe.

It never occurred to anyone that the Rev./Mr. D's week-long holy harangue was anything but true. After too many days of hearing pagan positioned as part of popular parlance, I determined to stand against this holier-than-all, them-vs.-us philosophy. Late one night, alone in my room, I created a six-panel cartoon. Initially, I wanted only to vent my rage. There was no grand plan to publish, posterize, or proliferate these dangerous doodlings in any way.

I showed the cartoon, first, to my brother and then to my mom and dad. There was no sense on my part that I had created anything mean or inappropriate. My family loved the cartoon. They thought it clearly stated the issues at hand. Most importantly, they were not offended by it.

"What are you going to do with it?" My dad believed it needed broader exposure.

"I'd like to turn it into a T-shirt, but we're not allowed to wear T-shirts to school."

This was the 1960s, and the school had an extremely specific dress code. Students at Mountain Christian Academy were outwardly indistinguishable from Mormon missionaries and Disneyland employees.

"What I really wish is that I could print it in the *Mountain Echo.*"

"Why *not* put it in the school paper?" My mom enthused. "You're the editor, aren't you?"

"It's not that easy. Every article, every cartoon — everything — has to run a gauntlet of approvals by faculty and administration. It wouldn't get past the principal's secretary." I was sure of that.

"Try it," my dad offered, in his familiar matter-of-fact way.

My father knew that whatever came of submitting this cartoon, at the very least chief among those who most needed to see it were the very administrators in the approval chain of command.

"Take it through the front door!" he affirmed. "If you start showing it around — on the sly — to classmates, eventually the administration will see it and call you in for more of their yakety yak." (That's how my dad referred to B.S.)

I liked the fearlessness of my dad's "front door" strategy.

"What if it really pisses them off?" I worried.

"If the shoe fits." My dad was more often coining his own phrases than using old clichés, but here, it fit. "If this makes them mad, or uncomfortable, then it is about them."

"But it is!" I exclaimed.

"Yes, it is. But will they see themselves in it?"

A plan was hatched. The birth of a notion.

I knew there were rough waters ahead. No doubt the usual list of administrative suspects would join the battle and I would be, once again, on the front line. Everything submitted for publication must carry the author or artist's name. My name was on the cartoon.

I had also written an editorial on our ever-wilting school spirit. Mrs. Pool—advisor to the paper—liked what it said, "Strong, direct, and positive." She suggested it be on the front page. The headline would be "Ardent Loyalty."

Mrs. Pool always waited to wade through each issue until all assignments were in and I had read and initialed each one. Then I did a small thumbnail sketch of the layout and placed it all in a folder for her to take home to read and initial with her approval. She always offered a few editorial suggestions, but there had not been any real battles over content.

There was also a piece by sophomore class reporter Mark Lo introducing two new mid-year transfer students. Mark's first draft mentioned one student hailing from "Sacred Heart (Catholic) High School" and the other from "Los Altos High School." I suggested for consistency he should clarify Los Altos High just as he had with Sacred Heart. I never told Mark what words to use, but Mark sat through those five days of chapel with everyone else. In Mark's next draft, there it was, "Sacred Heart (Catholic) ... " "Los Altos (pagan)." That's how it read when I put it in the file for Mrs. Pool, along with my soon-to-be legendary cartoon.

Everything came back approved. Everything. No comment about the cartoon or the "(pagan)" high school reference.

"This is going to be a big issue," Mrs. Pool said. "You know we send this out to board members, pastors, and other interested friends of Mountain Christian. Very impressive."

All text was typed directly onto paper printing plates. Then I drew the illustrations, cartoons, and hand-lettered headlines — directly on those paper plates.

For anything to end up in the paper it had to make it past me, Mrs. Pool, the principal's secretary, and MCA's director of development. I knew someone would stop it. We spent a week producing that edition of the *Mountain Echo* — typing, drawing, printing, collating, stapling. It was distributed on campus and mailed to area church leaders on a Friday. When I took it home, my family was very proud — of the whole thing. We had no sense that this story had just begun to be written.

That weekend at the Wilsons rolled along as normal as any other Saturday and Sunday. But there echoed through Northern California's Santa Clara Valley the ringing of phones in the homes of administrators and school board members. Apparently, the shoe fit a lot of feet. There were hardly enough shoes to go around before it was over.

Monday morning, before the administration could organize a response, the phones in the office were melting. Students shared conversations that they'd had with their parents — especially parents who taught in pagan schools. That one word in Mark Lo's article provided an opportunity for students to recount Mr. Davidson's entire chapel series to their parents — if they hadn't before. Those teacher/parents were not amused. Some were amazed we got it in the school paper. Me, too.

Of my friends who shared reactions to the cartoon, none said that their parents were offended. The shoe was not

CIVIL DEFENSE: Shelter revisited   BY Craig Wilson, Esq

TOO YOUNG TO KNOW

PARENTAL GUIDANCE

CHURCH'S INFLUENCE.

CHRISTIAN EDUCATION

Ready for the world!?

"...but be ye transformed by the renewing of your mind..."

ROM 12:2

11-22-67 Craig Esp.

their size. Many did see themselves in my cartoon and called school that Monday.

Then the school called my dad.

"I'll be right there." He dropped whatever he was doing and drove the ten minutes up highway 17 to our campus in Los Gatos.

The meeting started without me—my dad recounted it to me later in some detail.

"Have you seen this?" The principal held up the back page.

"I saw it a month ago when he first drew it."

"Doesn't it offend you?"

"It's not about me." Quiet confidence.

Who is it about?"

"Haven't you talked to the artist?" assuming they'd started with me. They usually did. "Why don't you ask him."

Is he talking here about Mountain Christian?" Mr. D badgered.

121

"If the shoe fits..." He zinged.

"Meaning?"

"I don't see myself in the cartoon, so it doesn't offend me." He couldn't believe he had to explain a cliché.

"Your son goes to this school, he attends a particular church, and you are his father. He's writing about those institutions so he must mean—"

"Yes, and not all churches, schools, and families are alike." He explained—probably quite slowly. "So, let's get him in here to speak for himself."

Moments later, I joined them: Dr. Woods (principal), Mrs. Pool and the Rev./Mr. Davidson (vice-principals), and my dad.

"Who are you talking about when you show parents, church, and school?"

"Just that," I said. "The influence parents, church, and school can have on us."

"But what are you trying to say about them?"

It was an interrogation. My dad's silence suggested he knew I could handle it.

Mrs. Pool was puzzled. "How could you do this cartoon and also write this great piece about school spirit?"

"They don't contradict each other at all. There's low school spirit here. Maybe the environment here isn't something to be real spirited about."

"How did this get into the paper!" Mr. Davidson was trying to accuse me of subterfuge.

"The same way everything else does," I said. "I put it in the 'Read & Approve' folder and Mrs. Pool took it home, and read it—I assume—along with all the other articles."

"I don't remember seeing the cartoon," she said.

"I promise it was there. Mr. Burley even called me out to print shop to redraw the cartoon on a printing plate.

It had to have been touched and seen by at least three administrators."

"That doesn't matter now," Dr. Woods interrupted. "It's been printed, it's out there."

(Later they found the entire folder in the office with Mrs. Pool's initials on *everything*.)

"Dr. Wood, I don't expect you to endorse or defend this. It's my cartoon. It's got my name on it. A lot of kids have told me about great conversations they had with their parents over the weekend because of this issue of the *Echo*—better than I could have hoped for."

"Well, it hasn't been great for us," Rev. Mr. D. again. "We're the ones answering all the calls."

"What kind of calls?" My dad wondered. "Supportive, angry, confused?"

"Parents, pastors," Dr. Woods explained. "Mostly angry."

"Of course," my dad said with a chuckle of familiarity. "In all my years as a school administrator, you usually only hear from angry parents. The ones who want to tell us how to do our job 'right.' Sometimes they offer helpful criticism. Sometimes their stuck in one of those bubbles from the cartoon."

"We end up apologizing for your stuff." Mr. Davidson, again.

"Please don't, Coach." I could not have been more sincere. "Just defend my right to think for myself, express my opinion freely, and claim the Apostle Paul's call that I quote in the cartoon, to be 'transformed by the renewing of your mind.'"

"Why would you want to criticize church, and school?" Mrs. Pool still trying to square my cartoon and school spirit editorial.

"I've attended six private Christian schools and visited dozens of others. I talk to kids I meet at games, speech meets, and music festivals, and we compare schools. Every school has rules—some more than others. Worse than the rules, at times, is the attitude behind them. Are we being protected, sheltered, held down or are we being trusted and encouraged to find all we can be in relationship with God? As for parents, I have friends at this school with fun, encouraging, alive moms and dads. Others are keeping their kids in straightjackets and mind vices. Their spirits are repressed; they are afraid to think for themselves. If their school and their church are that way as well, then of course, there is no school spirit, Mrs. Pool. Because there is no spirit."

"So this is about this school!" Mr. Davidson thought he had me.

"I described two different ways of being, Coach. Which one do you think we are?"

"You said we have no spirit here—"

"We have a negative spirit here, an oppressive spirit. We are taught about a God not of love, but of rules; of a black and white world where everything is Christian or pagan— good or evil."

"So that was your idea?" Dr. Woods asked, "The use of the word 'pagan' to describe a public high school?"

"No, sir! That's Mr. Davidson's philosophy." On this point, I was clear. "He preached for five days, an entire week of chapel on why Christian education is better than pagan education."

"I said public school." Mr. D was now very defensive. It was evident that this issue had been broached already.

"Excuse me, Coach, but on Monday of that week, you said 'public' maybe three or four times, and every time you said 'public or pagan schools.' Eventually, you used only the word 'pagan,' and you used it a lot!"

"I used the word, but not only that word."

"For four days you said only "pagan" over and over. Everyone was talking about it. Especially kids whose parents teach in pagan schools. They were really upset."

"That's not the point." Mr. Davidson was rewriting his sermon.

"Oh, I think that is the point, Mr. Davidson." Here at last, my father rejoined the discussion. "If you set up a world of us vs. them, you create enemies of friends. You've drawn a very small box around your world and only those who believe exactly what you believe can come in. Only those who follow your rules to the letter are welcome. You can't question the rules, you can't even talk about them. And, apparently, you can't even draw cartoons about them."

"There have to be rules. There has to be a standard," he argued.

"But why," I inquired, "must it choke us and drain our spirit? The Bible says, 'Where the spirit of God is, there is liberty'—except in Christian schools?"

"The Bible also says—" Mr. Davidson began.

"Are you really going to argue scripture against scripture?" I interrupted, feeling safer with my dad there.

"Where are we going with all of this, Bud?" My dad threw the ball back to his old friend Dr. Woods.

"Well, Wils, obviously this cartoon and the article referring to Los Altos High as *pagan* have created an uproar. We needed to know what motivated all this and how it got into the paper." We need to discuss this and decide on a course of action."

"A course of action?" My dad had no use for vagaries.

"Are you planning to punish me for my thoughts?"

The rest is silence.

Everyone had a lot more to say. Nothing was said. The meeting ended.

Outside the office, my dad said we'd talk at home. As I turned to head down the breezeway to class he called out.

"I'm proud of you!"

After the Storm

There was no further action taken. The discussion about my cartoon continued on campus not only in casual conversation, but even in classes. Off campus, the dialogue went on as well, especially in homes not represented in the cartoon — the ones outside the bubble. Shoeless families.

The approval system for the school paper tightened. I had made my point. I would never more succinctly and more publicly comment on the oppressive nature of life in the MCA world.

Autumn Arrives

The next year, Mountain Christian Academy moved to a new campus in the Santa Cruz mountains. Now the junior and senior high student bodies would be separated from the elementary grades. I would not have to worry about third grade teachers accusing me of spitting or dunking little kids' heads in toilets. (I was falsely accused of both early on at MCA.)

We also got a new fleet of teachers, including a creative writing teacher, who would be a personal boon to my early interest in putting thought to paper and folding phrases.

Gone was Mountain Christian's principal and founder, Dr. Woods. He had "resigned." More curious than his leaving was that the school-board-for-life offered the position of principal to my father! A family meeting was convened to discuss this weird blip in the universe.

Brother Friscus returned from his nightly walks with hood filled with walnuts.

For my father to step in at this point in the story would have heightened the drama. My father would want to modify and relax the severe fundamentalism of the school and that would have required drastic changes in philosophy and changes in administration and the make-up of the school board itself. In his proposal to the board, my father expected freedom to make whatever changes he deemed necessary to expand the growth and influence of Mountain Christian schools. (Besides the junior and senior highs, there were two elementary schools he would oversee.) Looking back, I'm not sure my dad really wanted the job. He would have given Mr. Davidson a year to see if they could work together. Eventually, though, my father knew that he would have had to let Mr. D go.

"A guy like that may never change," he would comment years later. That was as close to cynicism as I ever heard from my father. He believed anyone could change, improve, turn around.

(That's why very few names in this book are real names. In the long run this book is not about particular people, but particular problems born of belligerent behavior. If I used their real names I would leave out so many others who have and still are committing spiritual abuse. I hold out hope that the villains and bullies in these stories, who abused us, have changed, evolved, and relaxed their repressive ways. I have also used real names with my real heroes who "done good.")

My dad did not accept the position of principal, nor a follow-up offer to be on the school board. My dad loved the job we moved north to do—working with Christian nationals in twenty-two countries, many of whom had schools. He traveled to Guatemala, Liberia, Hong Kong, Sri Lanka, and Mexico to conduct teachers' training seminars. He had become a highly respected educator, internationally.

I became editor of the yearbook at the insistence of Mr. Campbell—the new history teacher and yearbook advisor. The battles there ensued on a weekly basis. This was to be MCA's first student-designed yearbook.

It didn't help matters when my own junior class selected as their "class verse" a quote from — wait for it — Henry David Thoreau!

If a man does not keep pace with his companions, perhaps he is marching to the beat of a different drummer.

We saw Jesus as our *different drummer.* I like that a lot. When we voted, it passed a gazillion to one. That "one" was a girl whose father was on the "school-board-for-life" and she, a young Brahman, had not thought for herself since the day she wore blue socks with a pink dress in third grade.

That Wednesday

One day, a Wednesday, in the first week of the second semester of my junior year, I was summoned to the office to discuss the number of Bible verses scheduled to appear in the yearbook.

"I know you won't be happy unless we put a verse on every page," I said, exhausted by this subject. "But it's not appropriate."

"Why not?" from Mr. D.

"We're not publishing a Bible!" (Steamed.) "The school brochure doesn't have a verse on every page."

"But," Mrs. Pool was there too, "we show the yearbook to potential students and their parents."

"The act of just pasting disconnected verses on every page trivializes scripture and says, *see,* we are good Christians, we must be, we have a little verse on every darn page," I said.

"It's clear that you don't agree with our philosophy on this."

"None of the previous MCA yearbooks have Bible verses on every page. Not even close. And they were all designed by Dr. Wood's wife!"

"It has become evident that you're not able to provide this school with the kind of yearbook we need."

"This is all about Thoreau, isn't it?" I had to know what was really happening. "Or am I finally being punished for my cartoon?"

"This is about the yearbook, son. We feel we need to make a change. So we're going to appoint a new editor."

It was 80–90 percent completed.

"We're going to give it to Aaron."

"He's not even a Christian!"

"He's a good kid and—"

"He smokes, swears, and hates this school."

"That's not fair."

"It's not fair to the yearbook staff," I said, holding back tears, "to reward months of hard work and sincere effort by giving them an editor who is brand new to the school, has zero experience in yearbook, and, frankly, is not a good kid."

"That's not a nice thing to say, young man."

"But it's true."

"We've made up our minds already. We're going to make the change."

"Well, it's almost done, so he can't do much harm." I didn't realize it at the time, but they took that as a challenge — like I was daring them to undo my design and theme.

"We do appreciate all the work you've done."

Before standing to leave, I knew this was my last day on their Mountain.

Leaving the Mountain

That night at dinner, in response to a "how was your day" question, I said, "I'm not going back to that damn place, ever!" (I rarely spoke that way.)

"What happened now?" My father set down his silverware to listen.

They knew the "Battle of the Bible Verse" story. I just told them the final chapter. When I got to "they're making

Aaron the new yearbook editor," every member of my family had a comment.

My father recommended I stay home the next day, Thursday, to think and pray about my decision to leave MCA. I stayed home all day.

My brother went to school as usual.

First thing Friday my mother and I went over to Oak Grove (pagan) High School, and I registered. It was a breeze. We then drove directly to Mountain Christian to withdraw. My dad's advice to enroll at Oak Grove before going up to MCA proved wise. We walked up the front walk into the center of the long building where the offices were. Chapel was in session, and from their seats in the large room at the end of the main building students and faculty needed only to turn their heads slightly left to see my mother and me arrive. (I was told later that a whisper billowed through the room, "He's leaving! Yes-s-s-s!")

Mr. Davidson slipped out of chapel, along the back of the building like a weasel ambushing his prey.

"Good morning, Mrs. Wilson. Would you two please step into my office for a moment?" He had a big grin on his face and his long basketball-scholarship arm outstretched with his bony hand gesturing toward his office. It was right out of Dickens. But now he was the Ghost of Educators Past.

I had already told the secretary I was there to withdraw.

"We have nothing to say to you, sir," my mother said, her voice trembling and angry. Given half a chance I believe she might have wrestled him to the ground.

"Just for a minute," he insisted. "Please."

"She said we have nothing to say!" I was just angry.

"Well, then ... ah, Mrs. ah, Pierce can give you the necessary forms." Mr. Davidson was trying to be helpful—I guess. "Will this be for Todd, too?"

131

"No," my mother said puzzled. "Todd has chosen to stay. Only he is leaving." Putting her hand on my shoulder.

The thought of one brother staying and the other one deciding to go did not register with Mr. Davidson. Seventeen-year-old "children," as he called us, were not capable of making such decisions nor should they be given the opportunity. But that is exactly what was happening.

"Fine," he said, and slithered away.

I cleaned out my locker and took my books around to each of my teachers to get their signatures on the release form. I was not prepared for the emotion in those brief and final encounters. Tears, hugs, big smiles.

"I'm so sorry," from one.

"We'll sure miss you," from another.

"Don't worry about this week's homework," with a grin and a tear.

"We'll never be the same without you."

"This is so wrong!" Then a big hug—from a male teacher. Men, in the church, in the 1960s, did not hug. Ever. (It's a little better these days.)

With all books returned, locker emptied, forms completed and turned in, I left Mountain Christian Academy—through the front door, as my father would say.

"Good-bye, McNair!" came a familiar yell from several voices out of many doors and open windows.

I turned to look and there, in the open door of a classroom, were most of my classmates, waving and throwing mock *Dating Game* kisses. "Good-bye!" several of them yelled. There was a long warm "Mountain Echo" that followed us all the way down the mountain.

I still hear it now and then.

That's Not Funny

As much as any memory in this book, my years at Mountain Christian Academy were the most difficult to recall and recount. I was fifteen to seventeen years old while incarcerated there. My parents and my faith got me through it. I knew back then that the Apostle Paul had settled the argument about a faith based on rules — "Legalism is helpless in bringing this about" (Galatians chapter 5 in *The Message,* by Eugene Peterson). I just kept hoping my overseers at Mountain Christian would read a little farther in their New Testament and be freed by Paul's encouragement.

My sense of humor that almost got me tossed off the mountain also got me elected student body president my first year there as a sophomore. My tendency toward the loquacious and obstreperous — then as now — kept me in the administration's crosshairs and guest chairs.

Coach Davidson also found occasion to enjoy my mimicking his bow-legged, bony-fingered, southern preacher style of coaching basketball, seeded with lots of misappropriated scripture verses, proclaiming the virtues of "Christian basketball" over "pagan basketball."

Mountain Christian was a difficult time. I have given it a large berth here in Captivity Harbor as it so vigorously represents that breed of fundamentalism I have too frequently butted heads with during my spiritual journey. It is far easier to tangle with theological zealots when they present themselves in the form of loudmouths and colorful characters. Jesus called the crooked church leaders of his day "snakes and vipers."

Radical religious extremism, zealotry, can be deadly to both body and spirit. Misguided zealotry can come from both the religious right as well as the religious left of any faith. Protestant extremists may not be crashing airplanes into twin towers, but they clutter the radio and TV airwaves driving home shallow, tangential agendas on everything from prayer in (pagan) schools to the evils of contemporary media.

What would be really radical and terrorizing would be a movement of true believers who took God and Jesus (God among us) at their Word. What if the radical new movement abroad in the land was collecting extra sweaters and warm coats from every household and handing them out to street folk. No Bible verse embroidered in the lining or clever tract, "The Lord Is My Fisherman's Weave Sweater," stuffed into the pocket?

Instead of telling our teens "don't, don't, don't," how about parents saying, "let's, let's, let's...do something together this weekend." And "let's" let the teenager pick the activity. Even if it's a rock concert. Be assured, they will not select the Stones or Billy Joel. Go anyway. Remember, it wasn't that long ago that your whacked-out "tastes" in wardrobe and music mystified and maddened your parents and you all lived through it. My folks survived Jefferson Airplane.

No one will be denied entrance into the Kingdom because of a cartoon drafted out of youthful frustration.

16

Previously, on a Much Smaller Hill, in Another Part of the Kingdom

A prequel to Christian mountain

> The bear went over the mountain.
> The bear went over the mountain
> The bear went over the mountain
> To see what he could see.
>
> —Children's song

There have to be rules. Such is the retort whenever I recount my adventures at Mountain Christian Academy. "You can't just allow teenagers to run free."

This is the black and white, turn or burn, good or evil thinking I grew up around. If you don't have a no smoking rule, people will smoke. Uh... no they won't. This world is full of people who don't smoke, don't chew, and don't go with girls that do. It is not an issue of faith; it is simple personal choice. It is possible to herd cats — and teenagers — without endless pages of ridiculously specific rules.

Witness Pacific Christian High School. A real place where I spent my freshman year. There was nary a day during my time at Mountain Christian that I did not fondly remember and long to be back at Pacific.

Nestled on a hilltop in the Highland Park area of Los Angeles, this non-denominational, church-related high school was academic home to the most diverse student body I was ever a part of in all my years as a student. It was snuggled between downtown Los Angeles, the bustling barrio of Hispanic East L.A., the ever-Asian Alhambra, elegant San Marino, and Pasadena — a town that runs the economic and ethnic gamut. Our campus had representation from all quarters — black, brown, olive, tan, befreckled, and the pigmentally challenged Euro-crowd were all there. We also had a goodly representation from "Churchianity's" many flavors, from a sprinkling of Free Methodists, to a chattering of Pentecostals, a committee of Presbyterians, an immersion of Baptists, a procession of Lutherans, and an unspecified number of non-denominationalists. There were even a couple of Catholics who found Pacific geographically desirable.

Mountain Christian, by contrast, was less colorful — colorless even — and more thinly denominational.

Another segment of the population that never was represented at Mountain Christian were the outcasts. One of the lesser publicized peculiarities of many private, church-related schools is that they take in laggards, rejects, and outcasts. These are the so-called "troubled teens" who teeter on the edge of society. The have not (yet) bumped up against the laws of the land, but have, meanwhile, been exiled from the bustling halls and ball fields of public schools that have given up on them and told them to "never come back." Private, church-related schools are their last, best hope — their only hope. Private, nonsectarian, college preparatory schools won't take them as they haven't the means and would drastically alter their image of "98.6 percent of our graduates go on to the best universities in the world."

We had six or so "challengers" (as my dad called them) at Pacific Christian. They were my classmates, teammates, and busmates. A few became friends. They kept things interesting for those among us who had bleached white bread for brains and knew that Jesus is the answer to *everything*.

You forget they are there. They melt into the student body. Then one day, a kid with a lit cigarette in his mouth cuts in front of you in line in the boys bathroom and you say, "That's not very Christ-like."

The line breaker looks over his shoulder, with cigarette dangling precariously from his lips, and says, "F--- Jesus."

Silence.

What would Jesus do, indeed?

Both the outcast and the stunned white-breader were good for the mix at Pacific.

You would expect there to have been a passel of rules at Pacific Christian to handle the homogenizing of the hostile and the holy. Guess again.

Other than the customary list of procedures and prescriptions governing attendance and dress code (even public schools had dress codes back then), Pacific had one big scary rule. It was more of a challenge actually — a line drawn in the sand of accepted behavior, informed by biblical faith and human decency. As close as I can recall it stated quite plainly: "As a student of Pacific Christian High School you are an ambassador for this institution and the biblical principles for which we stand. May your behavior reflect Christ's forgiveness and grace in all that you do and say, both on and off campus."

Wow.

Seems to me that that even covers spitting on teachers.

I loved being promoted to "ambassador," especially at age fourteen.

That was the first time I understood that as a follower of Jesus, my actions reflected on the teachings of God as others watched me. It was daunting and more than a little bit mystifying. Why is The Creator-of-the-World's reputation my responsibility?

Bermuda Shorts and a Necktie

With virtually no rules we didn't focus on the trivia of holding hands that would be the grand imbroglio at Mountain Christian. Dress code got much of our attention at Pacific and became our Maginot Line to be conquered. Girls were required to wear skirts or dresses every day and at a length that touched the floor when kneeling — that was the test. Guys could not wear blue jeans, but denim in various colors was okay. Nor could we wear a simple crew-neck T-shirt of any color or inscription to class. We could not wear our gym shoes in class, but we could change into another pair of tennies. Hair, for men, was to remain off the collar and above the ears and eyebrows. We all wanted to be John/Paul/George & Ringo, but not at Pacific. And not at most schools—public or private.

A couple of times each semester we'd have a "play day" where we could bring causal clothes to change into at lunch for an all-school bar-b-que before a big game or Homecoming. Even faculty "dressed down." (I think Mr. Saunders actually took off his tie one day and was able to teach math anyway.)

On "play days" our campus was more alive. Students were frisky and mischievous. If it was a game day. We were encouraged to wear play clothes in the school colors—red and black. We were the black panthers.

We also had "dress-up days," most notably for Spiritual Emphasis week—or, as I have long referred to it, "Be Kind to God Week." Those were "Sunday dress" days—nicer dresses for the girls, and ties, jackets or sweaters, and "church shoes" for the boys.

Some of us noticed that campus decorum was curiously more calm and quiet, civil and all-around polite on "dress-up days" and more raucous on "play days."

An idea was hatched that a handful of us took to our principal, the frighteningly quiet, though endlessly friendly, Mr. Harer.

"What if every Friday was a play clothes day? Call it Dress Down Fridays." This was 1966, decades before the now popular "casual Fridays" movement that swept through corporate cubicles.

Mr. Harer was decisive, but not an instant answer guy. Ever thoughtful, he sat back in his big principal's chair, pondered, looked out his window toward the giant eucalyptus trees that hugged our hilltop campus and then, leaning forward, he offered, "What if ever-other Friday was Dress Down and the alternate week was Dress-Up Friday?"

He liked it! Wow. And offered an actual compromise.

Stunned and delighted at his quick and open response, we looked at one another and — holding back victory dances—we said, "Sure. Great. It's a deal."

"Not yet. For now it's an idea," Mr. H cautioned. "Let me share it with the faculty and see if anyone balks."

Mr. H did make a proffer to the faculty and not all were enthusiastic, but none took a pugnacious position. By the time our plan was hatched and announced in chapel a few weeks later, everyone had heard about it. Almost no one believed it would ever happen, so as Mr. H explained it we beamed. I still think they should have carried us from chapel hoisted on their shoulders, but the many backslaps, handshakes, and shouted hosannas were none too shabby.

The Pacific Christian high school campus was a very different place every Friday. When we dressed up, we calmed down. When we dressed down we rowdied up.

Friends in my neighborhood who attended any one of three public high schools in Pasadena were stunned and jealous when they first learned of our unique Fridays.

Spending my freshman year of high school in the positive, open-minded, and often playful atmosphere at Pacific Christian spoiled me for life at Mountain Christian Penitentiary the following two years. I am sorry that my brother, Todd, didn't have a chance to experience Pacific firsthand. Even the public school I transferred to when I finally escaped Mountain was not as open and affirming as Pacific, though I am glad I finished my high school years in a public school.

Of all the pleasant and learning experiences that freshman year, why would I select such a trivial event as a dress code aberration to illustrate the good that was Pacific Christian High School? Aberration is precisely the point. You see there is little or no coloring outside the lines in Church World. More aptly put, there is no coloring outside the walls and electrified fences of church. For so many the only world is what exists inside church. Along the way friends and acquaintances who read many of these stories report similar, if not identical, experiences growing up in devout families of Jewish, Roman Catholic, Mormon, and every Protestant flavor. That church folk huddle in terror of the world beyond their dogma and narrow certainties isolates them from a world that needs to hear their message. Further, it divides them from one another.

English author, humorist, and Roman Catholic Christian G. K. Chesterton observed that "angels can fly because they take themselves lightly." People *don't* fly.

Have you noticed: churches, temples, and synagogues have parking lots rather than runways. But for a few brief shining moments there was a short but effective alteration in the life of Pacific Christian High School when, every Friday for a year, they offered flying lessons. In my year at Pacific Christian I never felt I was in captivity. Not once.

After ten and a half years in church-related schools, life in a public high school would be quite a transition—or so I thought.

That story next. Film at eleven.

17

Behind Enemy Lines
The move to "pagan" school

Impeach Earl Warren
—Bumper sticker, 1969

They'll crush him — like a bug! That's exactly what a kid at Mountain Christian Academy said would happen to me when I got to the public high school I transferred to in the middle of my junior year. It really didn't bug me. Stuff like that fed my contrarian sensibility and I set out to prove them wrong.

Oak Grove High School would not be my first foray into government-run education. I attended six weeks of summer school between seventh and eighth grades at the William McKinley government complex for pubescent humans, where I took speed reading, print shop, and self-defense.

Oak Grove High School in the Santa Clara Valley's southern region was a new school and an exciting one. I entered the second week of my second semester of my junior year. When I signed up for classes, I had so much of my college prep work done that I was allowed to cobble together a class schedule that looked more like summer camp than school. Drama, yearbook, commercial design, speech, biology.

Right quick I assessed the level of churchgoing students on campus. The only overt God-folk were a brother/sister act from my folks' church that took their stand for God by their vocal refusal to attend school dances and carrying Campus Life folders to hold their school papers. Campus Life is a national church-related organization (part of Youth for Christ) that holds in-home gatherings of students to discuss the spiritual/physical/mental balancing of life. They openly tackle moral and ethical issues that concern teenagers. One problem with carrying a Campus Life folder was that we had no Campus Life Club at Oak Grove High. The folders were a weak and meaningless gesture.

I planted my flag of faith in the ground by not carrying such folders or paper book covers with graphics of my faith, and I went to every dance and social event they had. I did not sit on the sidelines gawking at my peers bumping and flailing. I flailed along.

Within the first week, I became aware that the history and social studies department was a small army of folk a bit more to the left than my own political beliefs. I quickly acquired and affixed to my briefcase (the only hard case on campus) a bumper sticker proclaiming "Impeach Earl Warren."

At that time, 1969, Earl Warren was Chief Justice of the U.S. Supreme Court. He of the now-famous "Warren Report" that "investigated" the assassination of President Kennedy. Warren was a classic FDR-style liberal who ran an "activist" court that many believed was making law from the bench rather than defining laws against a Constitutional overlay of the founding fathers. My bumper sticker got the attention of the faculty phalanx of friends of the high court. They were enamored of my tenacity and awareness of second- and third-level political issues. They engaged me as a friend, though at times I felt like their mascot. They never talked down to me. That alone stood in stark contrast

Santa Claus
never died
for anybody.

As a freshman at the Minneapolis College of Art and Design I drew this in church—Park Avenue Methodist—one Sunday morning in 1970.

to the constant condescension of the Mountain Christian Academy administrators.

Just being engaged as a grown-up (even a partially-grown-up) was thrilling. At Oak Grove, they enjoyed my quick and knowing rejoinders. I even got three of them to admit during a lunch time debate that liberty, individual freedom, was a key and valued cornerstone of American life and that as state and federal governments expand, liberty diminishes. We are infantilized by the we-know-better-than-you-how-to-live-your-life laws being enacted by state, local- and federal governments on smoking and other personal choices.

Why the political rant? Because the government's belief that we need so many rules to help the masses of idiots about in the land is the same attitude that makes Mountain Christian Academy and so many other rule-bound institutions so debilitating to the human spirit.

The Creator gave us free will so that our love of our Creator would grow from authentic personal choice, not mechanical compulsion. We cannot fully enjoy life and health as imposed by federal or ecclesiastical mandate. Wars have been senselessly and unnecessarily fought over ridiculous rules and religious regulations. Even Jesus broke the massively nitpicky Mosaic law by "working" (healing) on the Sabbath.

I entered Oak Grove timid and worn down from too many senseless arguments where I was forced to defend being myself at Mountain Christian, a school that purported — even promoted — sharing my faith in the God of Free Will.

"Come now, let us reason together," wrote the profit Isaiah in the Bible's Older Testament. However, in too many churches, and church-related schools, their Isaiah says, "Come now, you're just a kid. Shut up and behave."

18

Magna Cum Bayah

Hundreds of retreats, not one advance

Where the giant mosquitoes roam...
—Sonny Salsbury

Every summer, there was summer camp. Still is. Campfire, crafts, horseback ridin', early-morning nature walks, cook-outs, watermelon feed, giant games, morning Bible hour, moonlit hikes, making out behind the archery hay bails, tug-o-war and other games we played only once a year. Down in the city we played Capture the Flag in Memorial Park with all the kids from the Pasadena YMCA. Camp was for unique experiences we couldn't have at home, like, Hide the Counselor—I've been both a hider and a seeker. "Hider" is funner. I have never been found at any camp where I was a hiding counselor. I always hide in the same location and I'll take my secret to my grave. Maybe I'll be buried in my secret spot.

Camp was always a place away—a retreat. Three times a year we would "retreat." I've been to hundreds of church "retreats," but not one "advance!" There was winter camp (a.k.a. snow camp), spring retreat, and summer camp.

Morning Bible study was "outdoor Sunday school" — singing, and a lesson. The advantage camp held over Sun-day school was that they had us five mornings in a row, and the rest of the day, to build on a theme. Depending on the speaker it could be fun, interesting, even entertaining, or as boring as Sunday school.

I once asked a favorite camp speaker if he had studied storytelling in Bible college.

"They didn't offer that," he told me. It had never even occurred to him that that's what he was doing. That was thirty years ago, and still storytelling and theatrical techniques are offered at few seminaries and church-related

colleges where ministry professionals are being trained. Maybe an M.Div. degree from seminary actually means mediocre delivery.

Along the road to Zion, I met and learned from a smattering of Bible teachers who kept the holy writ from becoming a homiletic wreck. The first truly engaging speaker/teacher that I recall was Bill McKee (real name) whose "Harley, Farley, Charlie, and Clod" made Shadrack, Mishack, and Abendigo from the Book of Daniel not merely palatable, but buoyantly befitting to young lives.

It was at camp, too, that I first encountered Bob Kraning (Kray'-ning), one of the most prepossessing preachers to youth the family of God has ever produced. He practices his propensity for preaching to all ages to this day. Bob could mesmerize, exhort, and regale all in one twenty-minute talk. He was the first church speaker I ever heard say, regarding communicating with youth, "If you can't say it in twenty minutes, don't get up to speak." Bob Kraning moved us. He nudged us toward eternity and we enjoyed the push.

The summers grew on, and finally I joined the ranks of summer staff (at the ripe old age of sixteen.) I spent a bunch of summers on the mountain learning from and laughing with the Reverend Mr. Kraning.

Enter Ben Patterson. A camp speaker (now a college campus pastor and highly sought after conference speaker), Ben dragged my brain, my intellect, into my pursuit of faith. He made my heart think. A friend once remarked of Ben's preaching, "It's obvious he reads the Bible and reads the newspaper." I knew that was the kind of minister Ben wanted to be. It's the kind of teaching that I had longed for all those years staring out the window of the Sunday school room at the driving range across the parking lot. Ben and I also became staff members together—at Forest Home

Christian Conference Center and later *The Wittenburg Door* magazine. Faith with a heart and a *mind* sounded more like God. In one of his many letters home from camp (to his friend James), Saint Paul wrote, "Faith without works is...boring." Actually, Paul said it was "dead." Either way it's just a useless concept.

Bill, Bob, and Ben were never boring. Never dead. They raised back to life the dead Bible characters—killed off by callow Sunday school teachers and pallid pulpits lacking trained storytellers.

Later, there were and are speakers I have been stirred, challenged, and entertained by: Tony Campolo, Ken Davis, Dick Gregory, Howard Hendricks, Roberta Hestenes, Becky Manning-Pippert, Juan Carlos Ortiz, Earl Palmer, George Regas, Mel White, and Jim Wilson (no relation.) All are true believers and practitioners of the fine art of rightly dividing the words of Truth. They are among the great tellers of the Greatest Story.

My hilarious and insightful friend Ken Davis says making the word of God boring is a crime. Let the incarcerations begin!

19

The Big Chat

What is a great relationship worth?

You talking to me? Are you talking to me!

—Travis Bickle (Robert DeNiro), *Taxi Driver*

For more than fifteen years after I graduated from high school—and following a year at Minneapolis College of Art and Design on a full scholarship, my parents kept at me to "finish school." If I moved to a new area, they asked, "Have you looked into any schools in that area?" When I'd change jobs, they'd ask, "What about getting back to work on your degree?" Or, "A few classes here and there...it all adds up." All their comments added up to a steady, fifteen-year-long din of annoyance. Their ceaseless harangue was not just conversation. They sent newspaper and magazine articles about college credit for what you've done in life. They might as well have sent matchbook covers announcing: "Earn a college degree at home." Whatever happened to "Draw this pirate, get a degree?" It was like having a small child incessantly yanking on your sleeve.

Relentless!

With all that sleeve yanking, eventually I was sleeveless, but they kept poking and prodding. I came to believe that my tombstone would one day bear the epitaph, "Never got his college degree."

They must have thought they were helping.

They were not.

A wedge was being driven between us that ultimately sapped my desire to call home, even to say hello or share a new joke with them, for fear they would ask, in passing, "Looked into any schools yet?" The rift over this issue was so tense that even when I did look into getting back at the books, I didn't tell them for fear they would turn up the heat.

My mother always wrote to me, from the time I first went away to summer camp, and she always included newspaper and magazine articles that she knew I would enjoy. I loved that about her. But too many of those articles outlined alternative methods of gaining a college degree. Those were the ones that blunted me—and our relationship. I cannot begin to adequately represent the depth of the anger I felt because of those comments and their steady stream of junky mail. The more my parents "helped" me, the more they hurt my feelings. I actually went back to school a couple of times in my adult life, and always enjoyed it. At one college, I was invited to be an instructor in the theatre arts department and my Chinese history teacher asked why I was even in school. "You don't need a college degree," he said.

"Will you write a note to my folks?" I asked him.

The "finish school" theme suggested that somehow I was unfinished, incomplete in my parents' eyes. I was deficient to the tune of one A-1 (or B.A.), all-American, bona fide, college degree.

Their love for me in so many areas of my life was rich, deep, and unwavering. But in this area — finishing college—they had a blind spot. It was as if they loved me unconditionally, on one condition: get your damn degree!

The Story

I moved to Orlando in 1982 when my street theatre — SAK Theatre — was hired to perform year 'round at EPCOT Center, Walt Disney World. During a much-needed reorganization, I was promoted from village idiot to artistic director, making me one of three principal owner/directors of SAK Theatre. This promotion carried an expansion of my authority and a big, fat raise.

Parallel to our reorganization, I was doing a bit of personal housecleaning—meeting with a therapist fortnightly. He was a left-handed Episcopal priest, with the surname Wilson. Our conversations focused on the attitudes and fears that were stopping me from getting on with my life more powerfully. We did not uncover any long-buried secrets of abuse. Instead, it was the conscious memories of my parents' regular comments that echoed into my present and reminded me not to "laugh too loud" (don't have more fun than anyone else) and "prove yourself" (just because you did a great job last time, doesn't mean you won't screw up this time). The interpretations were my own, but when you're told to "prove yourself" every time you enter a new setting, you begin to believe that they didn't believe you would always be able to do that.

Throughout my life, I heard a seemingly uninterrupted litany of phrases that were repeated with staggering regularity. At first they were playful chidings. Code words, if you will, for "we love," or "we're so proud of you." (They did say those phrases as well. Consistently and a lot.) They were all stinging paper cuts to my soul.

I believed they were meant to keep me in my place—stop me from going too far, too high, too successful, too much. The church has never quite been able to strike a balance between the important biblical teachings on humility while living in equipoise with all the God-given abilities we're all born with. How, then, do I not be "too much" while also being fully me? Trust me, "fully me," the *Full McNair,* is a lot. The church seemed clear—as were my parents—that a modicum of me would be sufficient.

One day, leaving the house to spend the summer on staff of a large church-related conference center, my mother hugged me, kissed me, whispered a prayer into my ear, and sent me on my way with, "Prove yourself."

"No!" I announced. "This time I've decided to be a complete and utter failure! I'm gonna be the worst thing that ever happened to them. They will send me home and you will be embarrassed in front of the whole world!"

"Oh, honey," she laughed, "don't say that."

"Well, don't tell me to 'prove myself' as if there's really some chance that all of a sudden my brain will fall out, my personality will dry up, and I'll turn into some beige-brained Bible boy with nothing to offer except an empty eagerness to serve Jesus by scrubbing sweaty horses."

"You know I pray for you every day," she answered.

"Give me a break, Ma!" (I called her "Ma" in character as in "top of the world, Ma.") "Don't pray for me one day a week, Tuesdays let's say. Just give me Tuesdays off to screw up on my own."

I hoped she might hear my pain, if only for a moment.

"Do you really need to remind me to 'prove' myself, as if there's even the slimmest chance I'd forget to be me?"

"I just don't want you to—"

"You don't want me to get into trouble for being who I am. I know. You're afraid that I'm gonna get it in the shorts like you did for being talented."

That was it! That's what the "complete college" articles were all about. Both my mom and dad had not finished their college degrees. My dad came within a handful of units of getting his master's, and my mother was studying speech pathology and theatre when her studies were interrupted by World War II. Even so, she taught school and was a brilliant speech therapist, drama coach, playwright, and director. But she never got her degree. I'm sure she missed some opportunities without a BA. Still, she was accomplished and highly esteemed in her field.

Through my counseling sessions with Barclay Wilson in Orlando, it became clear that I needed to confront my folks about some of this luggage I had been hauling around for far too long. A letter or phone calls would not do the trick. We would need to have a day of intense conversation about who I had become — or had not been able to become — as a result of their odd form of backhanded encouragement. Adding to all this parent stuff was the church's demand that I *fit in* and color inside *their* lines with the approved, muted colors. The church has always cast out the unusual because they did not understand it, whereas just the opposite was true with my mother. She knew. My mother knew, from her own experiences, the difficulties that could arise out of being even a bit different, unless you could sublimate your abilities into some useful function within the church: pianist, song leader, bus driver, Bible teacher (but only to children if you're a woman).

Over several months, I came to realize that I had chosen to be frozen, to live by my parents' words and "Churchianity's" restrictive, non-scriptural legalism. Now I was choosing to ignore and move beyond all that. It wouldn't happen quickly, nor easily. I fight it to this day!

My parents' unfulfilled dreams were not *my* unfinished business!

It was time to talk to them about this. In person. The Delta non-stop from Orlando landed in Burbank without event. My folks and I were glad to see each other, as always. I hadn't even told them exactly why I was coming to L.A., except to ask them to be available for dinner for the three evenings that I would be there. I imagined the first night would be the most difficult, breaking the ice on breaking the chain of conditions to their acceptance of the adult me.

The Chat

I was in my early thirties, and it was time to get on with my life. I wanted my mom and dad to be a part of that.

"I've been in counseling for the last few months. I'm dealing with my fear of success that I had thought I was over," I said at dinner. They listened. They didn't know that I had been in counseling, ever. No one in my immediate family had ever been in counseling for anything.

The churches that I grew up in had more than a healthy disdain for the world of psychological counseling. The church's aversion rose mostly out of ignorance rooted in a Byzantine notion that Jesus was the answer to . . . everything (except auto repair). They believed that a confused life was not an elaborate psychological and emotional condition. You simply needed "to get right with God." Fortunately, my family did not share this bewildering fear of counseling. That I was working with a cleric—albeit an Episcopal priest—did not hurt.

"Why do you think that you fear success, honey?" My mom asked sincerely. I think that fear of success was a new concept for her. I had been raised in a home where we tried anything, everything. Can you say "mixed messages"?

Failure, following an honest attempt, was never condemned at our house. A grade of "C" on a test or school paper was met with no reprimand or punishment, but encouragement.

"It comes from being told all my life that I was talented. 'You're a high potential, low achiever.' Then came the opposite, the clear signals not to shine too brightly 'cause 'they'll get you for being talented.'"

"Who said that?" My mother was amazed that I would take such advice to heart.

"You did! A lot." It was time for directness without hostility. "As far back as I can remember, you've told me the story about your high school drama teacher who was jealous of you and wouldn't cast you in the lead role of the school play, but gave it, instead, to a less capable girl, to spite you. I've never forgotten your words of warning. 'Watch out. People will be jealous of you because of your talent.' I've been afraid all my life to be the best." By now I was in tears.

So was my mother. "That story was about *me,* not you."

"You made it my story, Mother, and it has been my life. You warned me, more than once, that people would not like me because of my abilities. But just the opposite has been true." My anguish was not a little vague. "In every instance I was afraid of the pressure. Should I do a great job, the best I can? Or just good *enough* to be appreciated, but not some side show prodigy?"

"You really thought that?"

"I *live* that. How good should I do without being too much. And that almost always means not being fully myself."

"I'm so sorry, honey." My mother really was caught up short by all of this. I never intended to put her on the spot. I never believed she meant to harm me with her story, but to arm me against potential harm that she believed would inevitably come my way.

"I just wish you'd told me that being talented was a great gift from God and also carried with it great responsibilities, and that it's worth all the hassle."

"I just wanted you to do a good job, that's all," she explained.

"That's it, just do a good job, nothing more? The church never wants us to do a *great* job. No masterpieces, please. We're Christians." I wasn't interested in blaming my folks for all the indiscretions of Churchianity when it came to squelching talent, intelligence, and passion. "But you said it, Ma, over and over and over—*prove yourself.* As if there was actually some possibility that I might not. You seem to hold an outside chance that one day, unannounced and unexpected, my brains and spirit would leave me. You intimated that my creative marbles would inevitably fall out and roll behind the refrigerator where no one could get to them."

"You know we're very proud of you," my father added. "We believe you are capable of great things."

I think my father believed that, deeply, honestly.

"Remember when I was twelve and I auditioned at the Pasadena Playhouse for a big, professional production—on my own?"

"—and we let you go."

"No, you *encouraged* me to go, knowing that I really wanted to be in a big stage production that didn't have shepherds and papier-mâché sheep for once!"

"Do you think we don't treat you like that any more?" my mother asked.

"I think that you believe you're encouraging me when you send me stacks of brochures and magazine and newspaper articles about finishing my college degree."

"Is that what this is all about?" my dad jumped in.

"Not *all* of it. It isn't just about college. It's about you believing in me, with or without a college degree."

"We do believe in you."

"You have a very funny way of showing it. Every envelope with another tidbit on how to finish college at home is anther sigh of a disappointed mother and father who believe that eventually I will probably not amount to much of anything. It hurts. It hurts a lot and it has hurt for a very long time."

"We don't want to hurt you." My dad really did not understand how his brand of helping me was hurting me. "It couldn't hurt you to have something to fall back on, could it?"

"I'm not planning on falling in any direction, let alone back." I loathe that phrase, and had told him so, often. As an educator, he valued a solid educational underpinning. "I've been away from college for more than ten years now and have supported myself and lived comfortably. In fact, I was just given a substantial raise in my salary."

I told them the exact dollar amount of my new salary. "One of the articles you sent me, Mother, about the vibrant new Los Angeles Theatre Center mentioned their artistic director, who has a master's degree. His annual salary is six thousand dollars *less* than mine. So, I should drop everything to get a degree to fall back on less? And I don't want his job. I know it's not all about money." In fact, I grew up in a home where the cost was never the value of anything. We didn't live life, as my mom would say, with a price tag on everything we had.

"You might just learn something back in school." My dad didn't want education to go completely undefended.

"I'm sure I would, but whatever happened to 'Don't let going to school get in the way of your education?'" (a favorite phrase of my dad's during his decades as a school principal).

"Can you see or even imagine how the years of articles and words to 'check into colleges in your area' might feel like unconditional love with one big condition? We love you, BUT...."

They both reiterated that they sincerely wanted the best for me. We talked in some detail about my personal and professional goals. They mentioned as a way of putting my monetary success into perspective that my new salary would be more than their combined incomes. I was embarrassed for having mentioned it, but they said it was good I had since it made the point quite powerfully as to just how exasperated I was.

"By the by," I asked my dad, "how close did you ever get to completing your master's degree?"

"A few units and a thesis to write." He said it as if he'd gone to the market and forgotten to pick up bananas and a newspaper.

I pounced. "Have you checked into any of the colleges in your area? You know, a few courses here and there, and they all add up. Before you know it, you'd have your degree."

(Pause)

My dad had a smirk that was legendary when he had pulled a "gotcha." This time, though, the gotcha was on him.

"Is that what I sound like?" he asked rhetorically.

"Exactly!"

"Man, I would have smacked me long ago for saying all that." My dad was now vividly aware of the nuisance this had been to me. "I don't think I'd like somebody sending me a bunch of articles pushing me to finish my master's. I'd probably have to hurt 'em." He was big, but gentle.

Finally some long-overdue laughter.

"We just want you to be happy," from my mother.

"I am delirious with happiness. I've got a great job, lots of friends, I'm healthy, in a terrific church, and a homeowner."

They both assured me—in no uncertain terms—that they were proud of my accomplishments and that the deluge of educational ephemera would cease—not just taper off. I did not actually expect their reaction to be so positive, so non-defensive, so...absolute. Nor could I have ever guessed that their resolve would be so thorough. It was a gift from God. As we prayed together—in the middle of the meal—I knew what I had known all my life—that they were a gift from God, and that they loved me.

We finished dinner. The conversation would continue the following evening.

Chat, Night Two

"What shall we talk about tonight?" My mother asked playfully and cautiously.

"Women," I announced.

Looking up from and setting down his menu my dad struck a you-have-my-complete-attention pose.

"Do you realize," speaking mostly to my mother, "that all my life, whenever I brought a girlfriend or a date to our house or introduced her to you in public, you looked at her and said, 'You're gorgeous—What are you doing with him?' And pointed to me? Every single time."

"You always had very beautiful girlfriends."

"Yes, I did."

She snapped. "I was just kidding."

"It was funny the first eighty-three times you said it. Now it only hurts. I still date beautiful, witty, smart, interesting women, but I'm afraid to introduce them to you anymore. I have come to believe that I don't deserve them—at least you don't think I do. Beauty is too good for me. I feel, somehow, deep inside, that I not only don't deserve it, but that I'm getting away with something."

"Honey!" My mother thought I was exaggerating.

"No, I have actually been in the middle of a wonderful evening—candlelit dinner, terrific conversation, and been struck by the thought, 'Who do think you are, McNair? You don't belong with her. She's way out of your league.' "

Both of my parents smiled.

"It's true!" Again with the pleading voice. "You so convinced me that I don't deserve attractive women in my life and arms that it now terrifies me even to ask them to dance, let alone go out with me. Then when I do get up the juice to ask them out and they say, 'Yes,' I don't believe it. I think they're kidding."

They were quiet, intent. They didn't interrupt. When I finally paused to come up for air, my mother did not defend.

"I never meant to ridicule you."

"But you did. It belittled me and suggested to any lady I was with that she had bad taste, poor judgment, low self-esteem, or a combination of the three. If she couldn't do any better than me...."

"That's not at all what I meant," my mother said.

"That's what I heard, mother. You're the speech teacher. You know the rule: *the received* message is the message. I tried to take it all with a grain of salt. Then, one day I looked at this enormous mound of salt in the corner of my life."

"I'm so sorry, honey."

"Thanks, but I'm not here to make you wrong, just for us to see how critical we are to each other. It confused me. You are world champion parents. All my life, my friends loved you guys.

"It strikes me that this whole area of self-esteem has been completely missed by the church. God does want us to be humble, but humility was never meant to be self-loathing. How can I be all that God has created me to be, while, on the other hand, I am humble to the point of being embarrassed to use my talents and abilities? I'd never be able to audition for another play for fear that auditioning was boasting, showing off. I have met people who believe this. I spent a huge chunk of my life being terrified of my own gifts. I learned very early on that the church was about 'fitting in.' *Don't hurt the weaker ones by being strong.* Rather than encourage excellence and individuality, we squash it, flat, just in case we hurt somebody who's not self-propelled.

"What if, instead, we created a community of faith in which everyone was encouraged and supported in the development of their gifts, beauty, and personality? The church would become a community of the alive, vibrant, and tenacious. We could become, I believe, the place that people came to for affirmation, love, personal development, recovery, and empowerment."

Looking to my dad, a church leader, I asked. "Why don't we do that?"

"It's too much work." He wasn't guessing. "We're lazy, and we're afraid to get involved in people's lives. The world has trouble with real people. What makes you think that the church will be able to take them on any better?" He was right. But the family of God is supposed to be for everybody.

"It's like teaching school," my mom jumped in. "The biggest challenge to a teacher is the bright student, the talented one, the one with the most potential or even moderate potential, but great enthusiasm and curiosity."

"You're right," my dad continued. "We don't want to think about that stuff in church. Institutions are designed to be effective by treating the lowest common denominator."

"But why?"

"It's just too much work," my dad said, "to operate individually."

"When they asked Jesus what the greatest commandment was, he told them to 'love God, the Lord of your life, with your whole being.' Then he added, 'And the second is just

like it: Love your neighbor as much as you love yourself.'
How do we love our enemies as much as ourselves if we
don't first love ourselves?" I asked.

My dad agreed. "We have done a very poor job in the
church when it comes to figuring out self-esteem. We don't
even try."

Moving On

I'm not sure whether I went through all of this for them or
for me. I am quite certain that it was well worth the pain
and anguish that attended my trip home.

The conundrum that danced before me as I journeyed to
California for this summit of the heart and soul of me was
how my folks would listen and respond to all of this.

Have you ever wanted something so much that you knew
you would never get it, and then, when you did, you didn't
know what to do with it? This was such a time. I recommend
this for any relationship worth saving.

What's a Great Relationship Worth

No matter what my parents said or did, it was always my
choice to believe and live by it or reject it. It's about me
taking responsibility for me.

After my visit, there was a complete and dramatic change
in the way we related to each other.

I no longer worried when I called home that they might
ask questions about returning to college. So thorough and
direct were our conversations on the first two evenings that
we spent the third day reacquainting ourselves with who we
were at that moment. We began a new and healthier way
to talk and listen to each other.

As a card-carrying member of the Dramatists Guild of professional playwrights I could not have scripted these evenings any better.

For want of any relationship, we hold on to a bad one because we fear that confrontation might make a bad relationship worse.

Any relationship worth having is worth fighting for. Hard.

"Love is gentle, love is kind," the Apostle Paul tells us (1 Corinthians, chapter 13). But love that holds back the pain of a misfunctioning relationship is an unkind love.

I took on the myth of my own inadequacies in life and love to avoid confronting my parents and thereby hurt their feelings. It is astounding to me that I did not cry "uncle" years sooner. I knew, but only then realized, that Jesus died not only for what is done, but for things left undone!

There's another, better life awaiting us if only we will make the choice to go after it.

The remaining years of my parents' life were worth all the pain and false starts it took to complete my relationship in those three days in L.A. I never again let a comment from them go unexplained.

We never discussed college again, and my mom often seized the opportunity to tell a beautiful women I was with, "You are gorgeous—how lucky for you to be dating my son!"

20

Three Point Sermons
Of Christian basketball, street theatre, Cowboys and Indians

Keep them out of pool halls—and worse!
—Prof. Harold Hill, *The Music Man*

Our church always had a basketball team. Most churches did. Many churches have a gymnasium. Our church had an open-air basketball court.

In church, the pastor preached every Sunday, using passages from all over the Bible, but no matter what his text or subject, it was always organized into an outline of three easy-to-follow points.

One year the Venture for Victory basketball team came to our echoing quadrangle of sport and we all learned a new "three-point sermon"—gospel basketball. They played an exhibition game against our church team. The main exhibit was how weak our team was. (In the ensuing years we brought in local Christian college teams.) Venture for Victory was a college-level basketball team that played around the world. Even though VfV were all of the Caucasian persuasion, they were superior to our local Caucasians.

During halftime, instead of gospel pom-pom girls or finalists in the gospel dog Frisbee-catching contest, they brought a microphone to center court and, one by one, members of the Venture for Victory team told the story of their relationship with God. One player had spent all his life dreaming of playing basketball on a scholarship (why don't they call them basketballships or jockships?) at a big university and then being drafted by a pro team.

"Before Jesus, basketball wasn't the most important thing in my life, it was the only thing!" He had received several college offers, turning every one down in favor of a seat on the Venture for Victory bench.

His teammate told of forgoing a spot on the U.S. Olympic basketball team to "play for Jesus" in crowded gymnasiums in Europe, Latin America, and beyond. "Playing on this team is a greater victory than an Olympic medal." He seemed to believe it. I remember commenting to a friend at the time, "Get the medal, then people will listen."

Being a top athlete meant living to the fullest potential that God had created in you. To turn around and in the name of that Creator give up the chance to be the best was confusing to me. Eventually, I thought it was wrong.

The persistent message of the church was that whatever I do, make sure it has some use to the church. The assumption, of course, was that if you serve the church you serve God. God gives us mercy, unencumbered love, and eternal life. The church gives us perfect attendance pins, gold stars, and eight minutes in the program to do special music or "one of your little skits."

Couldn't a top athlete testify to her faith in God from a stronger position and to a wider audience in the athletic program of a major university? Kurt Warner, Super Bowl–winning quarterback of the St. Louis Rams, a Christian, would not have had as large an audience for his testimony of personal faith had he played for "Christians in Cleats" or "God's Gridiron" and traveled the countryside in a bus scrimmaging with Christian college teams from St. Paul to Waco to La Mirada. Indeed, Warner played in the obscurity of arena football prior to being horned into the Ram fold. While I am sure the tradition of gospel athletic teams has been effective in many lives, we will never know what might have come of all those athlete-Christians had they been athletes-in-academic-big leagues.

Good game, but they were sandlot sermons.

Twenty years after the first gospel basketballers came through our church, I was invited to speak at a conference in Canada where Canadian Football League (CFL) professionals invited a not-yet-Christian teammate for the weekend. Many related their own struggle to play pro ball or go into a ministry by coaching at a small Christian college.

I discussed the subject with several of these pro athletes one evening.

"In show business," I told them, "it's called 'playing to a bigger room.'" They liked that. They said they played to big rooms every weekend. I liked that.

Taking to the Streets

Big rooms were not always my stage. All my performing hasn't been with large professional theatre companies, though I have done that as well. Traveling in a street theatre troupe for a year performing comedies with a clear Christian message, we played campuses, mostly of large secular universities, including Stanford, UCLA, University of Colorado, and Berkeley — on the free speech steps of Sproul Hall. We played to enormous crowds of more than a thousand students. They were attracted, I believe, by our large colorful sets, medieval costumes, and stylized makeup (we applied on stage, before the show). Another attention getter was our use of broad comedy, freely punctuated with contemporary anachronisms. We peaked curiosities, and beat drums, and yelled "Play Today!" For many, it was a fellow student dragging you out of the cafeteria or away from the falafel cart that garnered a good chunk of our audiences. It should also be noted that we set up our 16′ x 20′ x 36′ high stage and colorful sets in the most heavily trafficked area of campus at midday, where there was always a crowd gathered. Our street theatre did not disappoint.

Our comedy was broader than any theatrical troupe of Christians I've seen before or since. Tight directing and heightened performance style held crowds for a solid forty-five minutes. The laughter was more often in billows and torrents as "Death" claimed another soul by a sharp slapstick clubbing on the noggin, or Noah observed that, with his three stoogey sons, "at this rate, it'll take us over a hundred years to finish this Ark." Our Satan was forever frustrated with inept demons.

During the period that I played Satan, I constantly found myself in post-performance conversations with students — and the occasional professor — who were amazed at how likable, enjoyable, and sympathetic my Satan was.

"Aren't we supposed to hate the devil?" asked one in a voice filled with irony.

"No. If the devil is completely unattractive, and detestable, we'd never listen to or follow him, getting ourselves into all this trouble." This rather straightforward logic often confused them even more. The whole idea is for an actor — even a Christian believer — to build the role to a point of actually "liking" the character. I relished playing Old Scratch.

169

Our show earned us "the right to be heard" with our deft comedy and production values. Getting an audience member to respond to God, personally, was a more personal, less public task.

More often than not we did not have to lead the conversation. Students would jump-start it by asking, "So, are you guys all really into Christianity? I mean, you're so funny!"

Like our brothers the gospel basketball team, we had opted to be a part of a traveling dog and pony show as a "ministry." Some of the actors and technicians I worked with had degrees in theatre arts from notoriously strong theatre schools. Others had been in schools with no formal theatre program. A few of us had worked in professional theatre. Some, surprisingly, had no theatrical experience at all. We did a lot of performances. In the fourteen months I was part of this company, we gave nearly three hundred performances of two different shows from Minnesota to El Paso, San Diego to Berkeley and all points in between.

Eventually, though, we could not decide if we were missionaries first, or theatre artists. After months of frustration with the company opting for "religious" choices over artistic choices, I asked, in a board meeting, "Are we actors or missionaries?"

It's a trick question. We were mostly theatre people who loved God and wanted to serve the Creator with our craft. Most of us had grown up in churchgoing families; many were the adult children of preachers and missionaries and were indoctrinated with the thirteenth commandment: If you must be an artist, be a *Christian artist,* for God's sake.

Too many in that troupe, and other "Christian theatre companies" I'd met, could not imagine themselves in a professional theatre company.

"I'm not good enough," they'd say. "They'll make fun of my faith." And, "Aren't there a lot of 'fairies and lep-rechauns' in the theatre who will drag me down morally?" These were real fears that I've heard from young actors in church and colleges. These are old fears based on lies told by the church for literally centuries. They are repeated in our private colleges and by clergy folk to keep talented people of faith from playing in the big leagues — the "big rooms." In the more than thirty years that I have been in the theatre, my experience has always been quite the opposite.

From my very first professional role in Shakespeare's *Richard III* at the Pasadena Playhouse at age thirteen, I re-member numerous occasions discussing my faith backstage with actors many years my senior. They knew I attended a private church school and they were curious. I have made numerous visits back to a professional theatre company I had been a member of, and close friends from that troupe have seen my one-man play on the life of Christ, *The Fifth Gospel.* We talked into the night about their reactions—artistic and spiritual. We talked about how I use my art to share my faith, while, at the same time, using the show to share my art with the church. So many of my theatre friends have expressed their admiration that I had fused my two passions in life—theatre and faith.

I have never been ridiculed for my faith by theatre folk, but I have often been criticized by church folk for being in the theatre. I even had a director offer to change the dialogue of my character because of a misperception on his part as to what I was willing to do and say on stage because I was a Christian. At my request, the dialogue was not changed—coarse as it was.

That day, when I asked for clarification of our self-image in the board meeting of the Christian-based street theatre, I was told that we were missionaries, first and foremost, and artists second.

At that moment, I knew I would have to leave. I was weary of the too many times that we needed to rehearse, but, alas, it was Tuesday and every Tuesday started with ninety minutes of Bible study and prayer.

I would plead, "We need the rehearsal time!"

I don't think they understood. Like so many other missionaries, they were martyrs, sacrificing personal dreams and well-being and family for the "cause." These young theatre martyrs were willing even to sacrifice or compromise their art. It was a great irony. Marshall McLuhan was right: the medium is the message and all too often, in the church, our medium is mediocrity.

More frustrating even than misguided loyalty to the ritual and tradition of our "Tuesdays with God" was the too many company members who had little or no experience or training for the work required on stage. One honest, well-meaning soul even came to us "because," he said (in a long Texas drawl), "I saw you guys perform when I was at the Naval Training Center and I always wanted to be in drama, so I thought, here's my chance." Argh! I remember asking our artistic director, following one particularly frustrating rehearsal, "If we were called *plumbers* instead of *players* and a guy showed up with no knowledge of pipes, wrenches, or basic plumbing, would we take him in simply because he said, 'I've always wanted to lie under a sink for two hours?'" He said we could train anyone.

It was here that our Christian zeal crippled us. More often than I care to recall, it kept us from excellence. Our shows were good; often they were great. They could have been great every time. We worked too hard for what we accomplished because we were at once rehearsing and teaching. We prayed when we should have rehearsed, and we pushed ourselves too hard when we might better have recruited more experienced artisans, instead of eager neophytes that were more hindrance than help.

Saint Paul's New Testament letter to James reminds that "Faith without works is dead." The exhausting pace of our work might have come from an insecure faith trying desperately to be shored up by works.

I believe there is room in God's family for the eager novice and enthusiastic amateur, but this was a professional theatre company, not Uncle Jesus' Skit Camp.

Whether dribbling the divine gospel of basketball or giggling the truth through street theatre, we have pinballed across the map hoping to make faith more appealing. The church has long believed that if we take the unappetizing tale of an ancient, crucified, pauper preacher and cover it with the frosting of athletic action or side-splitting comedy, we can finally get folks to listen to the Truth.

I don't know what became of all those Evangelical basketballers, but some of my street theatre pals were led by God to go into the professional theatre and are serving the Creator there now. Their faith remains strong and their shows are worth the price of a front row seat. The street theatre evolved into a strong and well-respected resident theatre company with biblical values at the heart of their work.

As a member of the national organization Christians in Theatre Arts (CITA) — I am actively engaged with believers who ply the boards of professional Christian theatre companies, academic theatre, and touring professional troupes. We also encourage and celebrate believers who work on Broadway, in regional theatres, and in film and television.

The smallest candle shines brighter in the darkest room.

21

Gospel Show Biz
If Tonto and Captain Kirk came to church

Happy trails to you, until we meet again.
— Roy Rogers, King of the Cowboys

As far back as I can remember, the church has had Christian entertainers: singers, magicians, chalk artists, athletes, ventriloquists, piano players, trombone players, radio personalities, weight lifters, karate teams, midget evangelists, actors, Christian cowboys, and Christian Indians. Eventually everything gets a Christian coat of paint like the thin candy shell on M & Ms—so there's no chocolate mess. Does making it Christian make it less messy? In the church, anyway, it makes it easier to swallow when it's poorly done.

My first church camp was a ranch and the promotional film was narrated by an actual singin' cowboy. Not Roy Rogers, but "Red" Harper. I met "Red" more than twenty years later. He really was a cowboy, and a warm, gentle human being. Roy Rogers was gentle too. (I met him, too!)

Christian celebrities come in three varieties: Those who are known to actually be Christians because they appear on TV or at your church; those who people say are Christians. (The church rumor mill always has a couple of hot new converts.) Finally, there are those who you think couldn't possibly be Christian because their lifestyle tells you they would never be invited to your church. ("I saw her smoking in a TV interview.")

Churches of all sects and denominations collect celebrities like bowling trophies. Celebrities draw a crowd. They make the church look good. Wouldn't you come to church if a big star like _____ (fill in most recent convert) believes in God?

Throughout my life, the church has been filling in that blank with names including: baseball's Bobby Richardson and Orel Hersheiser; singers Pat Boone, Bob Dylan, Johnny Cash, Noel (Paul) Stookey, various members of the Moody Blues, U2, and Earth Wind & Fire; former Nixon henchman Chuck Colson; TV chef Graham Kerr; authors Annie Dillard, Madeleine L'Engle, John Grisham, and John Updike; Senators Mark Hatfield and Paul Simon; and Presidents Jimmy Carter, Ronald Reagan, Bill Clinton, plus Bush 41 and 43. Some of these may surprise you. You are at liberty to amend the list as suits your theological curve and denominational proclivities.

Every president in my lifetime from Ike to "W" has been a "churchgoer," but few are claimed by Christian purists. Kennedy was Roman Catholic, Johnson swore and cussed, Nixon had Quaker roots (and feet of clay), Ford smokes a pipe, Carter taught Sunday school, and Mr. Reagan attended Bel Air Presbyterian Church in Los Angeles. George Bush (41) ended every speech with "God Bless the United States of America," but Evangelical Christians seemed only to claim him for military reasons. (Barbara Bush seems the ultimate pastor's wife.) Mr. Clinton attended a Methodist church in Washington presided over by a cleric who believed in *a lot* of stuff. Bush the Younger (No. 43) seems about as friendly with the Jesus of the New Testament as any Commander-in-chief in my lifetime.

Along the way the rumor mill fairly tripped over itself trying to come up with stories verifying the conversions of Eric Clapton, Leonard Bernstein, and Walt Disney—whose last words were decidedly not, "I go to prepare a place for you."

All this star collecting on the part of church folk is to make God look good. We sincerely, though foolishly, believe that folks outside the family of faith will say, "You mean to tell me Dean Jones, Bono, and Orel Hersheiser are all believers? That settles it! Sign me up!"

Naaaaaah!

People are smarter than that. True belief is a more personal, intimate choice than buying the same shoes that Magic or Michael wear, isn't it? Apparently the Glory of God just ain't enough. We parade the latest worldly wonders to be snatched from the jaws of Satan's deadly grasp.

In the midst of writing this, while surfing the too many channels of cable TV, I stumbled upon one of our more notorious husband and wife religious broadcasting teams (and their hair) with their guest, former Harlem Globetrotter cum preacher, Meadowlark Lemon. Thankfully, he was not dribbling for Jesus. The panel included an instrumental soloist. Following his very entertaining, contemporary arrangement of a familiar old hymn someone said — and I wrote it down immediately as it was such a remarkably indecorous statement, "Praise God for young people who use their talents for the Lord rather than playing in a nightclub somewhere."

The inference, of course, is that God-given talent used and expressed in a proficient and professional manner is not enough; it must be used in playing church music for a church audience. It's a spiritual ingrown toenail. The church spends far too much time entertaining itself.

To often, I have encountered church folk who, seeing me act in a Stephen Sondheim musical or Shakespeare play, ask if I've ever "considered using my talent for the Lord." Apparently it's "Use a paint brush, stay in church." Artists of faith must do art only about the stuff of faith—or such was, and still seems to be, the message of the church to the more actively creative folk.

Over the years, when people have suggested that I use my artistic abilities exclusively in the church, I haven't yet punched anyone in the nose who approached me with such a limited and narrow understanding of God's best intentions for me. I tell them that "ministry" for me is working at the peak of my ability—using my Creator-given abilities. Whether portraying the villainous Compte de Guiche in *Cyrano de Bergerac* or any of thirty characters in my own one man-play, *The Fifth Gospel,* I truly believe that the quality of my work is my testimony—my service to God. In the theatre, talking about doing our best work, we say "working at the top of our intelligence." That sounds like pursuing the Creator in me.

It took many years, though, to get past the layers of guilt that the church had spread over my mind if I would sing, act, design, write, or direct for anybody but the church. Their insistence on using only religious subject matter in the creation of art was claustrophobic, stunting, wrong.

Curiously, the church does not make the same demands of professionals in other fields as they do of artists. Of all the church folk I've met who sold insurance, I have yet to see one set up a little booth in the lobby of a church, or a church-going auto mechanic who confines his skills to church buses and cars of the clergy. Thankfully, not all schoolteachers of faith are working only in private church schools. That there are good teachers taking the Spirit of God into public schools portends hope for that most critical area of society.

We must take a long, hard, critical look at this compulsion for Christianizing everything from basketballs to paint brushes and guitars.

Eventually only the human soul restored and redeemed can become a child of God. Whether as athlete, actor, artist, accountant, or attorney, we show God's glory in the quality of who we are, not in what we are doing. Our dedication to the task praises God more than the task.

It is our passion to fulfill our Creator's grand design that pleases God.

The very first place we are told of God's Holy Spirit being given to a human being is not Moses, prophet and leader of his people. It is a remarkable passage in the Bible's second book, Exodus, chapter thirty-one, that begins: "God said to Moses, 'Behold I have given my Holy Spirit to Bezalel for working in gold and silver and bronze...and to all the craftsman....'"

Artists! The Spirit of Eternal God was poured into artists and craftsman to build the floating Temple, the Tabernacle that the Children of Israel carried through the wilderness. As you read on to the detailed account of all that God asked them to build, much of it had great symbolism. A whole lot of the Tabernacle design had no meaning; it was just there to be beautiful. It was art for art's sake. Art for God's sake.

22

Giving My Testimony without Moving My Lips

If the ventriloquist speaks in tongues, does the dummy share his gift?

It isn't easy being green.

—Kermit the Frog

There's always been a dummy in our family. We were not ashamed of this—we had other family traits about which to be embarrassed, and almost never were. I don't quite remember just when the first dummy showed up. There have been several. He sat at the dinner table, shared a bedroom with my brother and me, and even went to school and church.

He was a ventriloquist dummy and I was a ventriloquist. I still am, I guess, though these days I almost always move my lips when I speak.

As a kid in the 1950s, I watched TV a lot. We didn't have religious media watch hounds, with too much time on their hands, to tell us it was demonic and would turn us all into ax murderers and humanists. I turned into a ventriloquist. I watched everything: cartoons (*Mighty Mouse, Tom Terrific and Mighty Manfred the Wonder Dog, Flintstones,* and the best cartoon show ever, *Rocky and Bullwinkle*), sitcoms, variety shows, Roy Rogers, the Lone Ranger, and old movies—all of them. I was intrigued, early on, by anything with puppets: Howdy Doody, Bill Baird Marionettes, and Paul Winchell and Jerry Mahoney — with his friend, Knucklehead Smiff. (It was "Smiff," not Smith.) Every kid knew puppets were dolls brought to life by human puppeteers, but it was a way an adult could behave like a child. I remember the first time I heard Charley McCarthy go three rounds with W. C. Fields. If a little kid said those things, he'd have been spanked and sent to his room—in this case his suitcase. Charley always lived to sass again.

Using puppetry in the church was, for me, about having my own little theatre troupe where I was playwright, director, and cast. Ventriloquism was just the dummy and me. Every word out of both of our mouths was mine. We shared a brain. He was often smarter, quicker, and almost always, braver — more mischievous — than me. And, he was me. Everybody knew the "trick" but played and laughed along.

No one is really fooled, but at their technical best, all ventriloquists convince their audiences that the dummy is absolutely alive. Magic. In fact, in professional associations, ventriloquists are not members of the Puppeteers of America; they are in the Society of Magicians. They are illusionists performing a simple act of suspended disbelief.

I performed everywhere—schools (my own and others), churches, parties — and was available at the drop of a wooden jaw. I'd been on the stage since I was five, but the stage required other people. Puppetry, on the other hand, was limited only by the imagination of the puppeteer and audience.

I was also receiving a lot of attention for all my artistic pursuits. *Look what he can do and he's only (ten) years old.*

Fortunately, no act-your-age baloney was coming from my parents. They did suggest I not talk "so loud" once or twice.

My parents' concern was mostly about me paying attention to various creative urges and following them—after I had finished my homework. My mom and dad were cheerleaders for my brother and me pursuing our dreams. I can't honestly remember one time when either of them set limits of any kind on our curiosity and creative development. Along the way, numerous teachers and church folk offered plenty of corrective assistance. Most of their good intentions were a confusing nuisance.

One of my elementary teachers went to the principal—my dad—to inform him that he was raising me "wrong."

"Your son is very disruptive—the class clown!" thinking she was delivering shocking news.

The shock would be hers when my father said: "You underestimate him. More likely, he's the class circus."

I was not informed of this exchange until years later. My dummy said what people thought, but almost never talked about. In the church I grew up in, discussion on certain subjects just wasn't allowed. The dummy served as a conscience: making fun of the miserable record of our church basketball team or commenting on the color of the new choir robes. Regarding our annual Missionary Emphasis week, he once said, "Next week, a look back at the fashions of the last three decades."

The key: never be mean-spirited. Comedy can arise out of anger—humor as coping device. Humor can also teach, explain, fight back, and even heal.

I was quite young when I discovered the power of humor, not just through my ventriloquismatical pursuits, but from those earlier days as "class clown"—"class circus" being too limiting an appellation.

As a result, when I came up against an immovable object in the church, almost as quickly as I got angry about it, I got funny about it. As often as not funny preceded angry for me. Humor has been *a* device to assuage my otherwise obstreperous mien.

Even Jesus knew not to fight fire with fire. He tilted against the windmills of institutional power with wit, satirical stories, even stinging sarcasm. He referred to the religious leaders of his day as "snakes and vipers." Thankfully, Jesus chose metaphor over plainer, more coarse, direct language. He was a skilled storyteller, a ventriloquist, weaving his message into day-to-day lives of fishermen, farmers, and Pharisees. He aimed his remarkably powerful criticism at all of us via simple questions. We are still attempting to answer his more piercing inquiries.

Jesus was not the *answer* nearly as often as he was the *question.*

The role my dummy and I played in church was that of court jester, and conscience—the conscience of a child. We were the kid on the curb, watching the royal procession.

Everyone saw the same parade, but the dummy and I were the only ones who announced, "Hey, and forsooth, y'all, the king is in his boxer shorts!"

The dummy retired long ago, and I have taken up the holy cudgel in my role of jester. I'm still standing on the curb pointing out naked kings and prophets with fake I.D.

When I heard about the trouble Jesus got into for his strong criticism of hypocritical religious leaders of his day, I thought *if only Jesus had had a dummy to say those things,* he might not have gotten into quite so much trouble. Might there be bracelets that say "WWTDD?" (What Would the Dummy Do?) I wondered, too, what color they would print the dummy's words in all those Jesus'-words-in-red Bibles? Undoubtedly there would be some great sermons preached today on the words of the holy dummy. I would likely choose something Jesus' dummy had said to be my "life verse."

I learned early on that audiences remember what moves them, makes them laugh, cry, or get angry. Our attempt was to be slightly disruptive, more so than many had seen in church. I call it transgressive art. It is important to remember that all this was coming from someone who was young and *inside* the walls of institutional faith. This was a decade or more before the emergence of "Christian Comedians."

I never once turned the dummy around, showing my hand in his back, my fingers on the controls, and made the comparison to my relationship with God. My theology does not include a string-pulling, Geppetto-like God-as-master-manipulator, puppeteer. Plus, I wanted to maintain the sanctity of my art form. Dummies have dignity, too.

Either our performance was funny, quick, bright, professionally executed, thought-provoking, and just a little bit irreverent, or it was dull and ineffectual. Dull is an invitation to your listener to go, far, far away. Too much of what passes for performing art in the church these days is just bad performing with God's words pasted on as a "message" meant to justify or excuse weak writing or ill-prepared performance.

If nothing else, the audience would see God in the quality of our work. My art, indeed no one's art, should need justification, apology, or explanation. When we explain, we condescend and we admit to the weakness of our art. *Just in case you're too dumb to get it, this is what it's about.*

Too many performing artists in the church feel compelled to explain their work. Too many three-minute songs in Christian concerts have a two-minute introduction and are followed by a five-minute sermonette to explain it all. *I know my songs are shallow and you're stupid so here's the message.*

Art is Celebration

Art can enliven, engage, energize, excite, encourage, enrich, explore, and exalt. Otherwise, it is destructive: it can scar, spoil, and strip life of value and meaning. Much of church art these days is mere decoration—never venturing beyond ornamentation. Church art must be more than a beige spot on the soul. It is diminished—either by choice or institutional compunction—to sacred knick knack, Muzak, or hack art. There is bad art everywhere in the world, but too much of it done in the name of the Creator.

Christian painters may paint biblical subjects, but they should never be compelled to do so. When I speak of "bad" art, I do not mean there is no room for the novice, the beginner—of any age. Because the church relentlessly requires artists to be utilitarian, many artists who are true believers go elsewhere — outside the community of faith — to make their art apart from canonic decree.

Art is not an appliance. "Christian" is not an adjective.

Just as a guitar or piano cannot be a Christian, so too, a song cannot be Christian. It may speak of the stuff of faith, but there is no such thing as "Christian music." This goes for visual arts and performing arts, too. There is no Christian way to execute ballet, though I have seen enormously moving ballet done by Christian dance artists as a celebration of their faith. But we must never require them to be only sacred artists and thereby confine them to merely decorate our faith like so much evergreen and holly hung up for Christmas.

Our expressions of the Creator lived through our painting, poetry, and performance is art. Yes, people can and will see our eternal Creator, even through ventriloquism.

Art that is specifically sacred should differ only in its subject matter, but should still be executed with verve, tenacity, grace, and relentless craftsmanship. We will pay to see the fine art of Christians in the grand and intimate galleries of the world. That is the level of work our Creator intends us to create from our use of the gifts given us as a birthright. Less than that is lazy, embarrassing, ordinary, beige.

I have been all of these, too many times. I have also been excessive and disruptive. I will do them all again. I also intend to make exciting art, engaging theatre, and to scribe words that dance across the page and waltz into the heart of the reader. Don't be a dummy and make the artist-believer stuck in a ditch of church art. If you are an artist, paint, perform, and produce prose of elegance and magnificence that adds beauty, wonder, mystery, and exaltation to all of life. Paint with every color on the palette.

Flee the stifling halls of beigianity.

Grateful Acknowledgments

Say thank you.

—My mom

This began as a writing exercise and an attempt to exorcise some inner ticks. I needed to confront and smack around some old ghosts of growing up in a religiously addicted family. At the beginning of this process, I began sharing my musings with friends I had shared a pew with all those years ago. Unlike me, they left. Too many of them vacated their pew, but not their faith. Like me, they cherished God's grace, the gift none of us deserve and all of us need.

God's forgiveness is good, but too many of God's spokespersons were angry, abusive and stingy with grace, although it was not theirs to disseminate.

This book hopes to serve as a conversation with those who left and be an invitation for them to return. The community of faith, while still imperfect, has gone through a lot of changes. There's so much more to do.

Thanks, first, to Roy Mills Carlisle, of Crossroad Carlisle Books, who got excited about these stories when I read him the very first one—"A Confession."

To Tuvia and Sandra Vidan: Sandy — my right hand, my "Miss Preen," at Disney Imagineering — translated my fountain-penned paragraphs from paper to hard drive, giggling all the way. Tuvia (Ted), her Israeli-born psychotherapist hubby, was the first to call, and announced, "I don't know if you realize it, but you are writing about Jewish families!" That led to my showing my stories to Roman Catholic, Mormon, and ex-Lutheran friends. All were stunned at how my story was their story.

Judy Roberts found her story here, too. She, along with her roommate of thirty-six years, Wes, kept poking me toward completion. Judy and Wes are a cool and gentle breeze that blows regularly through my life.

A deep bow to my brother, Todd, who lived through most of this with me, but chose to be more silent with his consternation. If you see him, don't bug him about all of this.

Many others along the gospel trail read and encouraged these stories into print. Head of the pack is my pal Ken Davis, who affirms me in all I do with, "Just WRITE the darn thing!" (Always an encouraging spirit.) My pastor for nine years, George Regas, stretched me into new places with God that allowed me to write not out of anger, but passionate and smiling reflection.

There may never be an entire book on the glorious creativity of my mom and dad, but there should be. Their defense of my brother and me in our individuality pitted them against those who could have fired or maligned them—some tried. If home had been as restrictive and oppressive as too many churchacrats I collided with, I might not have been a churchgoer today. I certainly would not be in professional ministry were it not for my parents' unrelenting, palpable love. Though both died in 1992, their tenacious and inquisitive spirit supports me to this day.

A standing "o" to the tribe of teachers who allowed and corralled my Creator spirit even when it was disruptive. A few I fondly recall: Miss Hawthorne (grade three), Jack Green and Alice Lofgren (seventh), Ray Schweitzer (band master), Darcia Phillips (art), and everyone at Pacific Christian High School. At Oak Grove (pagan) High School, a deep bow to Frank Foehr (civics), Al Blair (drama), and John Aguilar (Design). Though not all shared my faith in God, their faith in me was tireless.

A small teepee full of characters employed and befriended me at their little mountain hideaway — Forest Home Christian Conference Center: Jim Slevcove, Ben Patterson, Sonny Salsbury, Bob Kraning, Wayne Rice, Mike Yaconelli, and the indefatigable Wes Harty. All continue to support and inspire.

Finally, a stack of crisp new two dollar bills to the host of waitresses, waiters, and management in scores of eateries across the land who allowed me to sit for hours—and often plug in my Mac—and stare off into my past. I always left cartoons on the napkins and butcher paper. "Can I get a fresh tea bag, please?"

McNair
Houston's Restaurant
San Francisco
Try the red Zin.
(March '3)

The Author's Story

Author, speaker, actor, director, playwright, inventor, cartoonist, ventriloquist (retired), theme park designer, dancing Episcopalian, daydreamer, corporate encourager, and fountain pen user C. (Craig) McNair Wilson has been going to church (and doodling there) all his life. He collects hats (236 and counting), political campaign buttons (400+), snow globes, old musical instruments, and rubber stamps. He has performed his two one-man plays (*The Fifth Gospel, From Up Here*) more than fifteen hundred times (and still performs them). As a longtime contributor to the groundbreaking magazine *The Wittenburg Door* (now, *The Door Magazine*), he began satirizing the foibles of faith and its Pharisees in his early teens.

During McNair's ten years at Disney he was a concept designer at Disney Imagineering, serving on the first team for seven new Disney theme parks worldwide. He has also completed his next book, *YES, AND... Brainstorming Secrets of a Theme Park Designer,* the little book of big ideas.

McNair's keynote addresses and workshops on creativity and human potential — through his company, Imaginuity Unlimited — are sought after by professional gatherings from IBM to the Salvation Army.

McNair was born in Minneapolis and grew up in California. His professional career in the theatre began at age thirteen at the famed Pasadena Playhouse. He later worked with the Minneapolis Children's Theatre, Lamb's Players, Orlando Theatre Project, and the California Shakespeare Festival.

He was manager of Lloyd's Ice Cream Shop.

McNair is available for dinner most nights of the week.

An Illustrator's Story

Every illustration in this book began in one of McNair's more than 140 sketch books. McNair's previous tome, *Everyone Wants to Go to Heaven, But...*, was chock full of illustrations, cartoons, and graphics. He also penned and doodled *YHWH Is Not a Radio Station in Minneapolis* (1983). He also illustrated *Good Advice* by Todd Temple and Jim Hancock and Sonny Salsbury's *Freeze-Dried Songbook* (for backpackers). He has never illustrated any books by Al Menconi.

His cartoons have soiled the pages of *Rolling Stone, Leadership, Decision, Youth Worker Journal, Wired,* and *The Door* magazine (*www.TheDoorMagazine.com.*)

He lives in the baggage claim area of a major airport in the San Francisco Bay area.

He still draws in church every Sunday. "Yes, you may look in my sketchbook."

On the off chance that anyone should ever doubt CW's perfect attendance record, he had saved every Sunday bulletin from church since he was five years old. including inserts, sermon outlines, missionary emphasis week flyers, and Westmont College choir tour handbills. There need be no doubting his long dedication!

Websites mentioned and recommended in this book

www.McNairWilson.com
Sign up here for McNair's FREE monthly Internet newsletter. McNair's web spot on the info-bahn: speaking schedule, other books and videos.

www.AssumeBrilliance.com
Web home of Imaginuity Unlimited (McNair's company that teaches creativity and brainstorming to corporate and ministry teams).

www.TheDoorMagazine.com
"The world's pretty much only religious humor magazine."

www.cita.org
Christians in Theatre Arts, national networking organization.

www.TruthorFiction.com
My friend Rich Buehler's site to ferret out web rumors from truth. Don't believe everything you hear, read, are told (even by church and government leaders). Double check. This is a great place to start.